Achieve great Chemistry with CGP!

Let's deal with the bad news first: the new Grade 9-1 GCSE Chemistry courses are tougher than ever, so you'll need to be at the top of your game on exam day.

Here's the good news: this fantastic CGP book is absolutely jam-packed with all the exam-style practice you'll need — it even covers all the new required practicals.

And since you'll be tested on a wide range of topics in the real exams, we've also included a section of mixed questions to keep you on your toes!

CGP — still the best! ☺

Our sole aim here at CGP is to produce the highest quality books — carefully written, immaculately presented and dangerously close to being funny.

Then we work our socks off to get them out to you — at the cheapest possible prices.

Contents

☑ Use the tick boxes to check off the topics you've completed.

Topic C6 — Global Challenges

Mixed Questions

Published by CGP

Editors: Mary Falkner, Emily Forsberg, Paul Jordin, Sophie Scott
With thanks to Christopher Harris and Emily Howe for the proofreading.
With thanks to Ana Pungartnik for the copyright research.

ISBN: 978 1 78294 516 1

Page 110 contains public sector information licensed under the Open Government Licence v3.0.
http://www.nationalarchives.gov.uk/doc/open-government-licence/version/3/
Data to construct graph on page 110 provided by the JPL PODAAC, in support of the NASA's MEaSUREs program.

www.cgpbooks.co.uk
Clipart from Corel®
Printed by Elanders Ltd, Newcastle upon Tyne

Based on the classic CGP style created by Richard Parsons.

How to Use This Book

- Hold the book <u>upright</u>, approximately <u>50 cm</u> from your face, ensuring that the text looks like <u>this</u>, not ˢ!ɥ̄ᵀ. Alternatively, place the book on a <u>horizontal</u> surface (e.g. a table or desk) and sit adjacent to the book, at a distance which doesn't make the text too small to read.

- In case of emergency, press the two halves of the book together <u>firmly</u> in order to close.

- Before attempting to use this book, familiarise yourself with the following <u>safety information</u>:

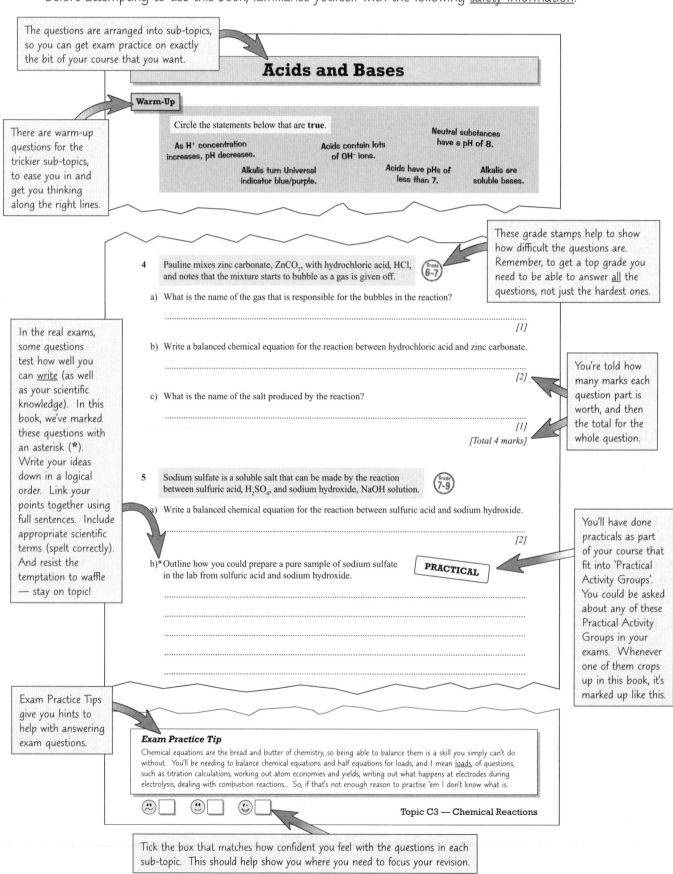

The questions are arranged into sub-topics, so you can get exam practice on exactly the bit of your course that you want.

Acids and Bases

Warm-Up

There are warm-up questions for the trickier sub-topics, to ease you in and get you thinking along the right lines.

Circle the statements below that are **true**.

As H^+ concentration increases, pH decreases.

Acids contain lots of OH^- ions.

Neutral substances have a pH of 8.

Alkalis turn Universal indicator blue/purple.

Acids have pHs of less than 7.

Alkalis are soluble bases.

These grade stamps help to show how difficult the questions are. Remember, to get a top grade you need to be able to answer <u>all</u> the questions, not just the hardest ones.

4   Pauline mixes zinc carbonate, $ZnCO_3$, with hydrochloric acid, HCl, and notes that the mixture starts to bubble as a gas is given off. (Grade 6-7)

a) What is the name of the gas that is responsible for the bubbles in the reaction?

....

[1]

b) Write a balanced chemical equation for the reaction between hydrochloric acid and zinc carbonate.

....

[2]

c) What is the name of the salt produced by the reaction?

....

[1]

[Total 4 marks]

You're told how many marks each question part is worth, and then the total for the whole question.

In the real exams, some questions test how well you can <u>write</u> (as well as your scientific knowledge). In this book, we've marked these questions with an asterisk (*). Write your ideas down in a logical order. Link your points together using full sentences. Include appropriate scientific terms (spelt correctly). And resist the temptation to waffle — stay on topic!

5   Sodium sulfate is a soluble salt that can be made by the reaction between sulfuric acid, H_2SO_4, and sodium hydroxide, NaOH solution. (Grade 7-9)

a) Write a balanced chemical equation for the reaction between sulfuric acid and sodium hydroxide.

....

[2]

b)* Outline how you could prepare a pure sample of sodium sulfate in the lab from sulfuric acid and sodium hydroxide.   **PRACTICAL**

....

....

....

....

....

You'll have done practicals as part of your course that fit into 'Practical Activity Groups'. You could be asked about any of these Practical Activity Groups in your exams. Whenever one of them crops up in this book, it's marked up like this.

Exam Practice Tips give you hints to help with answering exam questions.

Exam Practice Tip
Chemical equations are the bread and butter of chemistry, so being able to balance them is a skill you simply can't do without. You'll be needing to balance chemical equations and half equations for loads, and I mean <u>loads</u>, of questions, such as titration calculations, working out atom economies and yields, writing out what happens at electrodes during electrolysis, dealing with combustion reactions... So, if that's not enough reason to practise 'em I don't know what is.

☹ ☐   ☺ ☐   ☻ ☐

Topic C3 — Chemical Reactions

Tick the box that matches how confident you feel with the questions in each sub-topic. This should help show you where you need to focus your revision.

States of Matter

Identify which of the following statements is false. Tick **one** box.

Particles in liquids are free to move past each other but tend to stick together. ☐

When cooled, a gas can condense and become a liquid. ☐

There is hardly any force of attraction between particles in gases. ☐

Particles in liquids are held in fixed positions by strong forces. ☐

---

1 A chemical can undergo a physical change when held at different temperatures. It can also undergo a chemical change when reacted with other substances. **Grade 4-6**

Describe the differences between a physical change and a chemical change.
Give your answer in terms of the end product.

....

....

....

....

[Total 2 marks]

---

2 The particle model helps to describe the different states of matter. **Grade 6-7**

a) Give **two** limitations of the particle model.

....

....

[2]

b) Describe the differences between liquids and solids in terms of the movement of particles.

....

....

....

[2]

[Total 4 marks]

 ☐   ☐   ☐

The History of the Atom

1   Several theories of atomic structure have been
proposed since the start of the 19th century.

a) Describe the 'plum-pudding model' developed by Thomson in 1897.

....

....

....

[2]

b) i) Rutherford carried out the gold foil experiment where positively charged particles were fired at
       an extremely thin sheet of gold. Describe what Rutherford observed in his experiment.

....

....

[1]

ii) Describe the atomic model that was proposed by Rutherford.

....

....

....

[3]

c) Explain how Bohr's model differs from Rutherford's theory, in terms of electrons.

....

....

....

[2]

d) Explain why our current model of atomic structure differs so much from the older theories.

....

....

....

[2]

e) Peer review is an important part of developing scientific theories.
   New theories are critically evaluated by other scientists before they
   are published or accepted. Why is the peer review process important?

....

....

[1]

[Total 11 marks]

The Atom

1　Atoms are made up from protons, neutrons and electrons.

　a)　The relative mass and charge for the three subatomic particles are displayed in the table below.
　　　Complete the table by filling in the correct names for these particles.

Particle	Relative Mass	Charge
....	1	+1
....	1	0
....	0.0005	−1

[1]

　b)　State the **two** subatomic particles which form the nucleus and use their charges to explain whether
　　　the overall charge of the nucleus is positive, negative or neutral.

　　　...

　　　...

　　　...

[2]

[Total 3 marks]

2　The atomic radius is a measure of the size of an atom.
　　　It is approximately 10^{-10} m in length.

　a)　Which of the following pairs is **closest** in length?

　　　A　Atomic radius and nuclear radius
　　　B　Atomic radius and nanoparticles
　　　C　Atomic radius and bond length
　　　D　Nuclear radius and bond length

　　　Your answer ☐

[1]

　b)　Explain how the movement of electrons determines the atomic radius of an atom.

　　　...

　　　...

　　　...

[2]

[Total 3 marks]

Atoms, Isotopes and Ions

1   The table below shows some information about certain atoms.

Name	Atomic Number	Mass Number
Carbon–12	6	12
Fluorine–19	9	19
Neon–20	10	20

a) What does the atomic number of carbon–12 show?

    ....
                                                                                                    [1]

b) Calculate the number of neutrons found in one atom of neon–20.

                                                        Number of neutrons = ...
                                                                                                    [1]

c) State the number of electrons found in one atom of fluorine–19.

    ....
                                                                                                    [1]
                                                                                        [Total 3 marks]

2   Ions can have either a positive or a negative charge.

a) Describe what happens to an atom when it turns into a negative ion.

    ....
                                                                                                    [1]

b) Magnesium has atomic number of 12. Calculate the number of electrons found in one Mg^{2+} ion.

                                                        Number of electrons = ...
                                                                                                    [1]
                                                                                        [Total 2 marks]

3   Bromine has two main isotopes: Br–79 and Br–81.

a) Give the definition of an isotope.

    ....

    ....
                                                                                                    [1]

b) Bromine has an atomic number of 35. Calculate the number of neutrons in both isotopes.

                                                        Br–79 : .... neutrons

                                                        Br–81 : .... neutrons
                                                                                                    [1]
                                                                                        [Total 2 marks]

Topic C1 — Particles

The Periodic Table

1 Mendeleev was a scientist who developed an early version of the periodic table. Look at the diagram. It shows Mendeleev's Table of Elements.

H																
Li	Be											B	C	N	O	F
Na	Mg											Al	Si	P	S	Cl
K	Ca	*	Ti	V	Cr	Mn	Fe	Co	Ni	Cu	Zn	*	*	As	Se	Br
Rb	Sr	Y	Zr	Nb	Mo	*	Ru	Rh	Pd	Ag	Cd	In	Sn	Sb	Te	I
Cs	Ba	*	*	Ta	W	*	Os	Ir	Pt	Au	Hg	Tl	Pb	Bi		

Mendeleev's Table of Elements

a) Mendeleev left gaps in his table. Describe the reason why he did this.

He
....
....
....
[1]

b) Mendeleev used the gaps in his table to make predictions about the properties of elements that were still undiscovered at the time. Describe how the discovery of new elements in the years after Mendeleev published his table supported his decision to leave gaps.

....
....
....
[1]

c) Mendeleev tried to organise the elements in order of atomic mass. To get the arrangement he wanted, he then had to swap some of the elements round. Describe how the discovery of protons in the nuclei of atoms showed that Mendeleev was right to arrange the elements in the order that he did.

....
....
....
....
[2]

[Total 4 marks]

Electron Shells

1 The atomic number of neon is 10. *(Grade 4-6)*

How many electrons does neon have in its **outer shell**?

    A   2
    B   6
    C   8
    D   10

Your answer ☐ C

[Total 1 mark]

2 The atomic number of sulfur is 16. *(Grade 6-7)*

a) Write down the electronic structure of sulfur. ....2, 8, 86...

[1]

b) Draw a diagram to show how the electrons are arranged in a single sulfur atom.

[1]

[Total 2 marks]

3 Magnesium is found in group 2 and period 3 of the periodic table. *(Grade 6-7)*

Explain how you could use this information to **deduce** the electronic structure of magnesium.
Give the electronic structure of magnesium as part of your answer.

...........If its in group two it has two electron......
.......on the outer shell. and it has......
........3 shells if on period 3.......

....

....

[Total 4 marks]

Topic C2 — Elements, Compounds and Mixtures

Ionic Compounds

1   Sodium bromide, NaBr, is an ionic compound.

Sodium bromide conducts electricity when it is in solution, but **not** when it is a solid.
Explain why this is the case.

When solid they do not conduct electricity
or they are fixed in place, when in liquid
ions are free to move and carry an electrical
current.

[Total 2 marks]

2   Potassium has the electronic structure 2.8.8.1.

a) What is the charge on a potassium ion?

+1

[1]

b) What is the electronic structure of a potassium ion?

2, 8, 8

[1]

[Total 2 marks]

3   Calcium fluoride, CaF$_2$, is an ionic compound.

Draw a dot and cross diagram to show the bonding in calcium fluoride.
You should include the charges on the ions in your diagram.

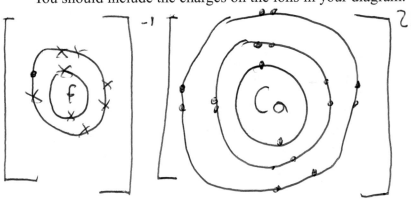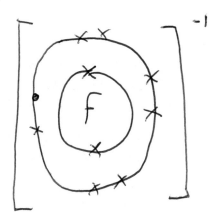

[Total 3 marks]

Topic C2 — Elements, Compounds and Mixtures

8

4 Sodium, magnesium, sulfur and chlorine are all found in period 3 of the periodic table.
Sodium and chlorine form the ionic compound sodium chloride, NaCl.
Magnesium and sulfur form the ionic compound magnesium sulfide, MgS.

(Grade 6-7)

a) Magnesium forms 2+ ions.
Use this information to work out the charge on the sulfide ions in magnesium sulfide.
Explain your reasoning.

All ions must be 0 so it mcy
2+ and its of Sulfur must be -2

[2]

b) The melting point of sodium chloride is around 800 °C.
The melting point of magnesium sulfide is around 2000 °C.

i) Explain why ionic compounds generally have high melting points.

They have a strong force of attraction
between then it takes lots of energy.

[2]

ii) The charges on the ions in sodium chloride are different from the charges on the ions in magnesium sulfide. Suggest how this difference leads to magnesium sulfide having a higher melting point than sodium chloride.

Sodium and Chloride adds ups to
1+ -1 so it not as strong as 2+
-2 thans why it a higher boiling

[3]

[Total 7 marks]

5 The elements strontium and barium both form ionic compounds.
Strontium and barium are both found in group 2 of the periodic table.
Strontium sits above barium in the group.

(Grade 7-9)

Predict whether barium is more reactive or less reactive than strontium.
Explain your answer in terms of loss of electrons.

the Strontium is be more reactive becau
barium has more shells so less force of
attraction between the nucleus so easier
to remove electrons.

[Total 3 marks]

Topic C2 — Elements, Compounds and Mixtures

Simple Molecules

1 Look at the diagrams. They show two different representations of the same molecule.

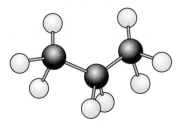

          Diagram A   **Diagram B**

a) Name the two types of diagram used here.

   i) Diagram **A** is a .....Ball and Stick......

[1]

   ii) Diagram **B** is a .....Formula diagram......

[1]

b) Suggest **one** limitation of the type of diagram shown in diagram **A**.

.....You canot see what the a elemen is on he ball......

[1]

[Total 3 marks]

2 The atoms of many elements can form covalent bonds.

a) Describe how covalent bonds give atoms a more stable electronic structure.

.....They are bonded together by strong Convalu bonds, they gain a full outer shell......

[3]

b) Neon has the electronic structure 2.8.
Suggest why neon does not form covalent bonds.

.....they have a full outer shell aready......

[1]

[Total 4 marks]

Topic C2 — Elements, Compounds and Mixtures

3   Silicon has the electronic structure 2.8.4.   (Grade 6-7)

Use this information to predict how many covalent bonds one atom
of silicon will form in a simple molecule. Explain your answer.

- will form 4 covalent bonds which
means because of the 4 electrons
on the outer shell.

[Total 2 marks]

4   Nitrogen has the electronic structure 2.5. Chlorine has the electronic structure 2.8.7.   (Grade 6-7)
Nitrogen trichloride, NCl₃, is a covalent compound.
In each molecule of NCl₃, one nitrogen atom is covalently bonded to three chlorine atoms.

Draw a dot and cross diagram to show the bonding in **one molecule** of nitrogen trichloride.
You only need to include the outer shell electrons of each atom.

[Total 2 marks]

5   Hashim says: "Covalent bonds are very strong, so you need a lot of
energy to separate the atoms in a covalent compound. This means
simple molecular substances must have high melting and boiling points."   (Grade 6-7)

Is Hashim correct? Explain your answer.

NO as simple molecules are very weak
forces so its not hard to change the states
so they have low and melting and boiling whereas
covalent bonds have strong forces of attraction
between them.

[Total 3 marks]

Exam Practice Tip

If you answered all these correctly, that's a pretty good sign that you know all about simple molecules and covalent
bonding. But don't forget, that's only half the story — you need to be able to compare simple molecular substances with
all the other types of structure covered in this section, such as ionic structures, polymers and giant covalent structure.

Giant Covalent Structures and Fullerenes

1 The diagrams below show two different types of carbon structure.

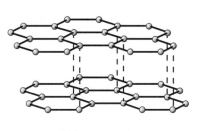

Diagram A

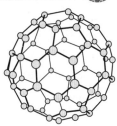

Diagram B

a) Name the two carbon structures shown.

i) Diagram **A**: ....Graphite..

[1]

ii) Diagram **B**: ....Fullerene...

[1]

b) Both of the structures shown are able to conduct electricity.
Explain why this is possible.

Only ~~three~~ three out of 4 carbon atoms
an outer shell free low of delocalised electron
that can move soit coducts same with cab
fullerene *[2]*

c) Which of the two forms of carbon shown would you expect to have a **higher** melting point?
Explain your answer.

....

....

....

....

[3]

d) Name **one** other type of carbon structure, and draw a diagram below to show its bonding.

Structure: ....Diamond.....

[2]

[Total 9 marks]

   Topic C2 — Elements, Compounds and Mixtures

Nanoparticles

1   Luca says "Nanoparticles are bigger than molecules. **[Grade 4-6]**
    One molecule on its own can't be a nanoparticle."

Which of the following **best** describes why Luca is **incorrect**?

A   Some large molecules contain hundreds of atoms, which
        makes them big enough to be classed as nanoparticles.

B   Some atoms are very large, so molecules consisting of large
        atoms can be big enough to be classed as nanoparticles.

C   A nanoparticle is any particle less than 100 nanometres
        across, so there is no minimum size for a nanoparticle.

D   Anything larger than a single atom can be classed as a
        nanoparticle, including single molecules.

Your answer ☐ A

[Total 1 mark]

2   Nanomedicine is the name given to the use of nanoparticles to treat illnesses. **[Grade 6-7]**

a) A scientist says "Nanomedicine could bring great benefits in the future."
    Describe **one** example of a possible use of nanoparticles in medicine.
    State what property of the nanoparticles you have named makes them suitable for that use.

    They can give bandage wraps that ~~influence~~
    has antibacterial properties to is a run in

[2]

b) Another scientist says "We should be cautious about using nanomedicine."
    Suggest why this statement might be considered correct.

    Havent been used sd before so heath
    concern and side effects may occur.

[2]

[Total 4 marks]

3   Explain how the small size of nanoparticles gives them
    different properties from larger particles of the same material. **[Grade 7-9]**

    Surface area to volume ratios av particle
    decrease the SA increase, Nano particles
    have a hight surface area to volume ratio
    different to larger ones.

[Total 3 marks]

☹ ☐   😐 ☐   🙂 ☐

Polymers

Warm-Up

The sentences below are about polymers. Use the words below to correctly fill in the gaps in the passage. Each word can only be used once.

Polymers are .....*long*..... molecules. They are formed

from .....*small*..... molecules called .....*monomers*..... .

Polymers are often referred to as .....*plastics*..... .

Polymers contain .....*covalent*..... bonds, but often behave

very differently from simple .....*molecular*..... substances.

long

covalent

molecular

plastics

monomers   small

1*   Look at the information below. It describes some properties of two polymers, Y and Z.

Polymer Y

- contains carbon and hydrogen atoms only
- high melting point
- rigid
- does not stretch

Polymer Z

- contains carbon and hydrogen atoms only
- low melting point
- flexible
- easily stretched

Suggest and explain the reasons for the differences in the properties of the two polymers. Give your answer in terms of the nature and arrangement of their chemical bonds.

....

....

....

....

....

....

....

....

....

....

[Total 6 marks]

Topic C2 — Elements, Compounds and Mixtures

Properties of Materials

1   Look at the table. It lists several compounds containing elements from group 7 of the periodic table.

Name of compound	Formula	Structure
iodine monochloride	ICl	simple molecular
potassium chloride	KCl	ionic
sodium fluoride	NaF	ionic
fluoroethane	C_2H_5F	simple molecular
poly(fluoroethene)	$(C_2H_3F)_n$	polymer

a) Which other compound in the table would you expect to be **most similar** to fluoroethane, in terms of its melting and boiling point? Explain your answer.

....

....

[2]

b) Bromine is another element in group 7. Under certain conditions, some compounds of bromine can conduct electricity. Other compounds of bromine exist which never conduct electricity.

Explain how it is possible for different bromine compounds to have different electrical properties.

....

....

....

[2]

[Total 4 marks]

2   The element phosphorus exists in several different forms.
Two of the forms of phosphorus are known as white phosphorus and black phosphorus.
White phosphorus is made of molecules of four phosphorus atoms.
Black phosphorus has a giant covalent structure similar to graphite.

Marcus predicts that black phosphorus and white phosphorus will have similar melting points, since they both contain only phosphorus atoms. Do you agree with Marcus? Explain your answer.

....

....

....

....

....

....

[Total 5 marks]

Topic C2 — Elements, Compounds and Mixtures

Metals

Which of the following are typical properties of a metal? Circle the correct answers.

good conductor of heat   brittle   high melting point   low density   malleable

low boiling point   poor conductor of electricity   crystal structure when solid

1   Which of the following **best** describes the properties of **most** metal oxides?

	State at room temperature	Result when added to water
A	solid	forms basic solution
B	solid	forms acidic solution
C	liquid	forms basic solution
D	liquid	forms acidic solution

Your answer ☐

[Total 1 mark]

2   Many properties of solid metals are due to their structure.

a) Draw and label a diagram to show the structure of a solid metal.

[3]

b) i) Explain how this structure means metals usually have high melting points.

....

....

....

[2]

ii) Explain how this structure allows solid metals to conduct electricity.

....

....

....

[2]

[Total 7 marks]

Topic C2 — Elements, Compounds and Mixtures

States, Structure and Bonding

1   Methane (CH_4) has a melting point of –182 °C and a boiling point of –161 °C.
    Water (H_2O) has a melting point of 0 °C and a boiling point of 100 °C.
    Methane and water are both simple molecular compounds.

Based on this information, which compound has the **stronger** intermolecular forces?

A   methane
B   water
C   both the same strength
D   can't tell from this information

Your answer ☐

[Total 1 mark]

2   Look at the table. It shows some properties of four elements.

Name	Melting point / °C	Boiling point / °C	Appearance		
			solid	liquid	gas
fluorine	–220	–188	colourless	bright yellow	pale yellow
mercury	–39	357	silvery metallic	silvery metallic	n/a
bromine	–7	59	red-brown metallic	red-brown	red-brown
rubidium	39	688	silvery-white metallic	silvery-white metallic	n/a

During an experiment, samples of each of these four elements were placed in separate test tubes.
All four test tubes were then gradually cooled together, from 25 °C to –200 °C.

Describe what you would expect to observe as the experiment progressed.
In your answer you should describe what will happen to each sample.

....

....

....

....

....

....

....

....

[Total 4 marks]

3　Look at the table. It shows some properties of six substances.

Substance	Melting point / °C	Boiling point / °C	Conducts electricity?
1	−190	−165	no
2	1500	2840	yes
3	761	1584	only if molten or in solution
4	1690	2815	no
5	−73	65	no
6	688	1367	only if molten or in solution

a) Leonie says: "Substances 2 and 4 have similar melting points, so they probably have a similar structure." Is she likely to be correct? Explain your answer.

....

....

....
[1]

b) Jing says "Substances 3 and 6 are ionic compounds."
Is she likely to be correct? Explain your answer.

....

....

....
[1]

c) i) Which substance is a gas at room temperature? ....
[1]

ii) What does this suggest about the structure of this substance? Explain your answer.

....

....

....
[2]
[Total 5 marks]

Exam Practice Tip
These questions are all about comparing the properties of different substances. You can use everything that you know about the properties of different structures to help identify unknown substances and also to choose the right material for a particular job. There are more questions about choosing suitable materials on pages 94-95.

  　Topic C2 — Elements, Compounds and Mixtures

Purity

1   Misty-Marie is doing a chemistry experiment.
    The instructions say she needs to use pure water.
    Stanley offers her a bottle labelled '100% Pure Spring Water'.

Grade 4-6

Suggest why Stanley's water is unlikely to be suitable for Misty-Marie's experiment.

....

....

....

....

[Total 2 marks]

2   A scientist is comparing two samples of the same compound.
    One sample is pure, but the other contains a number of impurities.
    The compound is a liquid at room temperature.

Grade 4-6

The scientist decides to work out which is the pure sample by heating both samples
and recording their boiling points. Explain how she will be able to tell which is the
pure sample, even if she does not know the boiling point of the pure compound.

....

....

....

[Total 2 marks]

3   The melting point of ammonium nitrate, NH_4NO_3, is 170 °C.
    The melting point of citric acid, $C_6H_8O_7$, is 156 °C.

Grade 6-7

An unidentified substance is found to have a melting point of 163 °C.
Which of the following **best** describes what this tells you about the unidentified substance?

   A   The substance could be impure ammonium nitrate, but isn't impure citric acid.
   B   The substance could be impure citric acid, but isn't impure ammonium nitrate.
   C   The substance could be either impure ammonium nitrate or impure citric acid.
   D   The substance could be a mixture of equal parts ammonium nitrate powder
        and citric acid powder.

Your answer ☐

[Total 1 mark]

Topic C2 — Elements, Compounds and Mixtures

Purification Techniques

1   Look at the diagram.
    It shows a set of equipment you could use for separating a mixture in the lab.

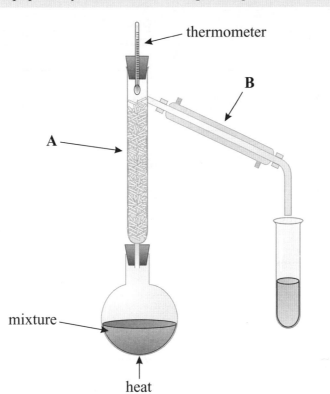

thermometer

B

A

mixture

heat

a) Name the pieces of equipment labelled **A** and **B**.

i) **A**: ....
                                                                                                            [1]

ii) **B**: ....
                                                                                                            [1]

b) i) What is the name of the separation method this equipment would be used for?

....
                                                                                                            [1]

ii) Describe what type of mixture you would use this method to separate.

....

....
                                                                                                            [2]

iii) Reuben is using this method to separate a mixture.
     His mixture contains a flammable liquid.
     Suggest a suitable piece of equipment that he could use to heat the mixture.

....
                                                                                                            [1]
                                                                                                [Total 6 marks]

Topic C2 — Elements, Compounds and Mixtures

20

PRACTICAL

2* A student wants to separate the components of a mixture.
The mixture is a white powder composed of barium sulfate, $BaSO_4$, and potassium iodide, KI.
Look at the table. It shows some information about the two compounds in the mixture.

Name	Melting point / °C	Boiling point / °C	Appearance at room temperature	Soluble in water?
barium sulfate	1580	1600	white solid	no
potassium iodide	681	1330	white solid	yes

Describe in detail a method the student could use to obtain pure samples of both compounds.

....

....

....

....

....

....

....

....

....

....

....

....

....

....

....

....

....

....

[Total 6 marks]

Topic C2 — Elements, Compounds and Mixtures

3 Sodium chloride dissolves in water, but not in ethanol.
Sodium chloride has a melting point of 801 °C and a boiling point of 1413 °C.
Ethanol has a melting point of −114 °C and a boiling point of 78 °C.

a) Suggest a purification method which would separate a mixture of sodium chloride and ethanol, but **not** a mixture of sodium chloride and water. Explain your answer.

....

....

....

....

[3]

b) Suggest a purification method you could use **either** to separate a mixture of sodium chloride and water **or** to separate a mixture of sodium chloride and ethanol. Explain your answer.

....

....

[2]

[Total 5 marks]

4 Look at the table. It lists the melting and boiling points of three compounds.

Name	Formula	Melting point / °C	Boiling point / °C
cyclopentane	C_5H_{10}	−94	49
cyclohexane	C_6H_{12}	6	81
ethyl ethanoate	$C_4H_8O_2$	−84	77

Suggest why a mixture of cyclohexane and ethyl ethanoate might be more difficult to separate than a mixture of cyclohexane and cyclopentane.

....

....

....

....

....

[Total 2 marks]

Topic C2 — Elements, Compounds and Mixtures

Chromatography

1   Which of the following **best** describes the mobile phase
    and stationary phase used in gas chromatography?

	Mobile phase	Stationary phase
A	viscous liquid	heated tube
B	unreactive gas	heated tube
C	viscous liquid	unreactive gas
D	unreactive gas	viscous liquid

Your answer ☐

[Total 1 mark]

2   The diagram below shows the chromatogram produced by
    analysing an unidentified substance using gas chromatography.

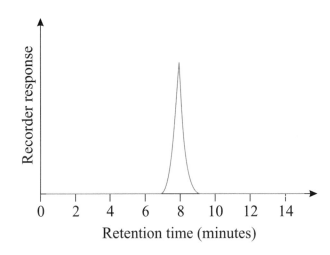

a) Explain why this chromatogram suggests that the unidentified substance is a pure chemical.

    ....

    ....

    [1]

b) In gas chromatography, what is meant by the term 'retention time'?

    ....

    ....

    [1]

    [Total 2 marks]

3   Olivia analysed an unknown mixture of liquids using paper chromatography.   **PRACTICAL**
     The chromatogram she produced is shown below.

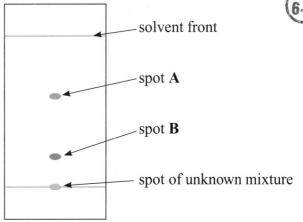

a)   How many component liquids does this chromatogram suggest are in the mixture?
     Explain your answer.

     ....

     ....
                                                                                                                                        [1]

b)   Calculate the R_f value of spot **B**. Use a ruler to help you.

                                                                               R_f = ...
                                                                                                                                        [2]

c)   Olivia is given a list of five chemicals.
     She is told that her mixture contains some combination of chemicals from the list.
     Explain how Olivia could use pure samples of the chemicals on the list
     to identify the components of the mixture using paper chromatography.

     ....

     ....

     ....

     ....
                                                                                                                                        [2]
                                                                                                                    [Total 5 marks]

Exam Practice Tip
There are a couple of quite different methods here — paper chromatography might be easier to get your head around,
especially if you've done it in class, but you need to know the details of gas chromatography too. Make sure you know
what 'mobile phase' and 'stationary phase' mean, and what the different phases are for each type of chromatography.

                       Topic C2 — Elements, Compounds and Mixtures

Relative Masses

1 Which of the following compounds has a relative formula mass of 62.3? **Grade 4-6**

    A   sodium chloride, NaCl
    B   potassium bromide, KBr
    C   magnesium fluoride, MgF_2
    D   sodium bromide, NaBr

Your answer ☐

[Total 1 mark]

2 The formula of the compound zinc cyanide is $Zn(CN)_2$. **Grade 6-7**

Find the relative formula mass of zinc cyanide.

relative formula mass = ...
[Total 2 marks]

3 The formula of the compound barium nitrate is $Ba(NO_3)_2$. **Grade 6-7**

Find the relative formula mass of barium nitrate.

relative formula mass = ...
[Total 2 marks]

4 An oxide of an element, X, has the formula X_2O_3. **Grade 7-9**
The relative formula mass of X_2O_3 is 159.6.

Calculate the relative atomic mass of element X.

relative atomic mass = ...
[Total 3 marks]

Topic C2 — Elements, Compounds and Mixtures

Molecular and Empirical Formulas

Warm-Up

The molecular formula of the compound pentanoic acid can be written $CH_3(CH_2)_3COOH$.

How many oxygen atoms are there in one molecule of pentanoic acid?

How many carbon atoms are there?

How many nitrogen atoms?

How many hydrogen atoms?

1 The compound butane-1,4-diamine has the molecular formula $C_4H_{12}N_2$. Which of the following is the empirical formula of butane-1,4-diamine? *(Grade 4-6)*

A C_2H_5N
B $C_2H_6N_2$
C CH_3N
D C_2H_6N

Your answer ☐

[Total 1 mark]

2 Look at the diagram. It shows the displayed formula of the compound dithionic acid. *(Grade 4-6)*

$$\begin{array}{ccc} & O & O \\ & \| & \| \\ H-O- & S-S & -O-H \\ & \| & \| \\ & O & O \end{array}$$

a) What is the molecular formula of this compound?
   Give your answer in the form $H_aS_bO_c$, where a, b and c are whole numbers.

....
[1]

b) What is the empirical formula of this compound?

....
[1]

[Total 2 marks]

Topic C2 — Elements, Compounds and Mixtures

3   Decaborane is a compound with the molecular formula $B_{10}H_{14}$.   (Grade 4-6)

What is the empirical formula of decaborane?

....

[Total 1 mark]

4   Compound R has the empirical formula $C_6H_5O_2$.   (Grade 6-7)
Each molecule of compound R contains 10 hydrogen atoms.

What is the molecular formula of compound R?

....

[Total 2 marks]

5   Oct-1-ene is a compound with the molecular formula C_8H_{16}.   (Grade 6-7)
Emmy says the empirical formula of oct-1-ene is C_2H_4.

Is Emmy correct? Explain your answer.

....

....

....

[Total 1 mark]

6   Compound Q has the empirical formula C_2HF.   (Grade 7-9)
The relative formula mass of compound Q is 132.0.

What is the molecular formula of compound Q?

....

[Total 3 marks]

Topic C2 — Elements, Compounds and Mixtures

Conservation of Mass

1   During an experiment, a student burns 4.7 g of iron metal in air to form 6.7 g of a solid oxide
of iron. The student claims that increase in mass has come from extra atoms being created
during the reaction. Do you agree with the student? Explain your answer.

Grade
4-6

....

....

....

[Total 1 mark]

2   A student is investigating a reaction between zinc and hydrochloric acid.
The reaction produces hydrogen gas and a solution of zinc chloride.
The student's experimental set-up is shown in the diagram below.

Grade
6-7

Conical flask

Hydrochloric acid

Mass balance

Zinc

124.568 g

a) How would you expect the mass of the conical flask and its contents
to change over the course of the reaction? Explain your answer.

....

....

....

[2]

b) The student repeats the reaction, but this time attaches a gas syringe to the top of the flask.
How would you expect the mass of the apparatus and its contents
to change over the course of the reaction? Explain your answer.

....

....

....

....

[2]

[Total 4 marks]

Chemical Formulas

Sort the elements below into the table to show the charges on the ion that they generally form.
You might want to use the periodic table on the inside back cover to help you with this question.

iodine   barium   sodium   magnesium

lithium   calcium   sulfur   selenium   chlorine

Charge on Ion			
+2	+1	–1	–2

1   Radium is in Group 2 of the periodic table.

What ion would you expect radium to form?
A Ra^{2+}
B Ra^+
C Ra^{2-}
D Ra^-

Your answer ☐

[Total 1 mark]

2   In an ionic compound containing just iron and chlorine, the ratio
between the number of iron ions and the number of chloride ions is 1 : 3.

What is the charge on the iron ion present in the compound?

Charge on iron ion = ...
[Total 1 mark]

3   During a reaction, an ionic compound containing magnesium and nitrate ions is produced.

Which of the following chemical formulas correctly shows the compound formed?
A Mg_3NO_2
B Mg_2NO_3
C $Mg(NO_3)_2$
D $MgNO_3$

Your answer ☐

[Total 1 mark]

Topic C3 — Chemical Reactions

Chemical Equations

1 Hydrogen gas is an important reactant, used in the Haber Process. It can be made, at high temperatures, using the following reaction.

$$CH_4 + H_2O \rightarrow CO + 3H_2$$

Which of the following word equations correctly describes this reaction?

A methane + steam → carbon dioxide + hydrogen
B ethane + steam → carbon dioxide + hydrogen
C methane + steam → carbon monoxide + hydrogen
D methane + steam → carbon + oxygen + hydrogen

Your answer ☐

[Total 1 mark]

2 Calcium carbonate chips were reacted with nitric acid at room temperature. The products of the reaction were water, a gas and a salt solution.

Complete the reaction equation by adding state symbols to describe the reaction.

$$CaCO_3(..........) + 2HNO_3(..........) \rightarrow Ca(NO_3)_2(..........) + H_2O (..........) + CO_2(..........)$$

[Total 2 marks]

3 Sodium metal can react with oxygen molecules in the air to form sodium oxide (Na_2O).

Write a balanced equation for this reaction.

....

[Total 2 marks]

4 Silver chloride, AgCl, can be made by reacting silver nitrate, $AgNO_3$, and sodium chloride, NaCl, together in a precipitation reaction.

$$AgNO_{3\,(aq)} + NaCl_{(aq)} \rightarrow AgCl_{(s)} + NaNO_{3\,(aq)}$$

a) How can you tell from the reaction equation that this is a precipitation reaction?

....

[1]

b) Write a balanced ionic equation for the reaction above.

....

[2]

[Total 3 marks]

Topic C3 — Chemical Reactions

5 In a chemical reaction, sulfuric acid and aluminium metal react to form hydrogen gas and a salt solution of aluminium sulfate.

Ben has written this equation for the reaction:

$$Al_{(s)} + H_2SO_{4\,(aq)} \rightarrow Al_2(SO_4)_{3\,(aq)} + H_{2\,(g)}$$

a) Explain what is meant by the symbol '(aq)' in the chemical equation.

....

[1]

b) Ben's equation is not balanced. Write a balanced chemical equation for this reaction.

....

[2]

c) Given that all the solutions involved in this reaction are colourless, use the chemical equation to say what would you expect to see happen during the reaction. Explain your answer.

....

....

[2]

[Total 5 marks]

6 Balance the following symbol equation to show how sulfur reacts with nitric acid.

$$S + HNO_3 \rightarrow H_2SO_4 + NO_2 + H_2O$$

....

[Total 2 marks]

7 Use the half equations below to construct a full equation to show the reaction between aqueous bromine and solid potassium to form potassium bromide, a soluble salt.

Magnesium half-equation: $K_{(s)} \rightarrow K^+_{(aq)} + e^-$

Bromine half-equation: $Br_{2\,(aq)} + 2e^- \rightarrow 2Br^-_{(aq)}$

....

[Total 2 marks]

8   Zinc reacts with tin sulfate solution as part of a redox reaction.
The full reaction equation is shown below.

$$Zn_{(s)} + SnSO_{4\,(aq)} \rightarrow ZnSO_{4\,(aq)} + Sn_{(s)}$$

a)   Write the ionic equation for the reaction above.

....

[2]

b)   Use your ionic equation to write balanced half-equations for the oxidation of zinc
and the reduction of tin in the reaction above. Use e^- to represent an electron.

Zinc half equation: ....

Tin half equation: ....

[2]

[Total 4 marks]

9   A student is carrying out a reaction in a lab that involves reacting
a solution containing silver ions, Ag^+, with solid copper.

a)   Write the balanced ionic equation for the reaction, using the half equations below.

Copper half equation: $Cu_{(s)} \rightarrow Cu^{2+}_{\,\,(aq)} + 2e^-$

Silver half equation: $Ag^+_{\,\,(aq)} + e^- \rightarrow Ag_{(s)}$

....

[2]

b)   Given that the only other ions present in the reaction are nitrate ions (NO_3^-),
write a full balanced equation for the reaction.

....

[2]

[Total 4 marks]

Exam Practice Tip

Chemical equations are the bread and butter of chemistry, so being able to balance them is a skill you simply can't do
without. You'll be needing to balance chemical equations and half equations for loads, and I mean <u>loads</u>, of questions,
such as titration calculations, working out atom economies and yields, writing out what happens at electrodes during
electrolysis, dealing with combustion reactions... So, if that's not enough reason to practise 'em I don't know what is.

Topic C3 — Chemical Reactions

Moles

1 What is the approximate number of atoms in 1 mole of carbon atoms?

    A 7.23×10^{23} atoms
    B 7.23×10^{24} atoms
    C 6.022×10^{-23} atoms
    D 6.022×10^{23} atoms

Your answer ☐

[Total 1 mark]

2 A pharmacist is synthesising aspirin, $C_9H_8O_4$, as part of a drugs trial.
After the experiment, the pharmacist calculates that she has made 12.4 moles of aspirin.
What mass of aspirin has she made?

.... g
[Total 2 marks]

3 How many atoms are there in 7 moles of ammonia, NH_3?
Give your answer to 3 significant figures.

.... atoms
[Total 2 marks]

4 The table below contains information about various atoms. Complete the table.
Where appropriate, give any answers to 2 significant figures and in standard form.

Element	Atomic Number	Mass Number	Mass of 1 atom (g)
Hydrogen	1	1	....
Nitrogen	7	....	2.3×10^{-23}
Aluminium	13	27	....
Argon	....	40	6.6×10^{-23}
Titanium	22	48	....

[Total 5 marks]

5 A sample of an unknown element contains 1.2044×10^{25} atoms. Grade 7-9

a) How many moles of atoms of the element are in the sample?

....

[1]

b) Given that the atoms have a mean mass of 9.27×10^{-23} g, what is the identity of the element?

....

[2]

[Total 3 marks]

6 A student is investigating an unidentified acid, which is made up of oxygen, sulfur and hydrogen atoms. Grade 7-9

a) Given that 3.5 moles of the acid has a mass of 343.35 g, what is the relative formula mass of the acid?

....

[1]

b) The percentage mass of the acid made up of oxygen atoms is 65%. To the nearest whole number, how many moles of oxygen atoms are in one mole of the acid?

....

[2]

c) In one mole of the acid, there is one mole of sulfur atoms. Deduce the chemical formula of the acid.

....

[3]

[Total 6 marks]

Topic C3 — Chemical Reactions

Calculating Masses

Complete the following sentences by filling in the blanks with the words on the right.

1) If the amount of limiting reactant in a reaction is decreased,

   then the amount of product made will ....

2) If the amount of limiting reactant in a reaction is increased,

   then the amount of product made will ....

3) If the amount of an excess reactant is increased,

   then the amount of product made will ....

not change

decrease

increase

1   James is investigating the reactivity of some metals. As part of his investigation, he places   **Grade 4-6**
     a piece of magnesium metal in a flask containing an excess of hydrochloric acid and
     monitors the reaction. The reaction produces hydrogen gas and a metal salt solution.

a) Which of the reactants is the limiting reactant?

   ....

   [1]

b) James repeats the experiment but changes the starting quantities of magnesium and acid.
   He lets the reaction proceed to completion, and notes that once the reaction has finished,
   the reaction vessel contains a small amount of grey metal and a colourless solution.

   In this second experiment, which of the reactants is the limiting reactant? Explain your answer.

   ....

   ....

   ....

   [2]

   [Total 3 marks]

2   An industrial process converts the alkene ethene into ethanol, according to the reaction below.   **Grade 6-7**

$$C_2H_4 + H_2O \rightarrow CH_3CH_2OH$$

What mass of ethanol can be made from 53.2 g of ethene, given that water is in excess?

.... g

[Total 2 marks]

Topic C3 — Chemical Reactions

3 The following equation shows the complete combustion of ethane in air.

$$2C_2H_6 + 7O_2 \rightarrow 4CO_2 + 6H_2O$$

a) Given that 128 g of oxygen were burnt in the reaction, what mass of water was produced? Give your answer to an appropriate number of significant figures.

.... g

[3]

b) A company burns ethane to generate power for an industrial process.

As part of a carbon-reducing scheme, the company can only produce a maximum 4.4 tonnes of carbon dioxide per day (where 1 tonne = 1 000 000 g). What is the maximum amount of ethane that the company can burn each day so as not to exceed the limit of carbon dioxide?

.... tonnes

[2]

[Total 5 marks]

4 Urea, $(NH_2)_2CO$, is a compound that can be synthesised industrially using the following reaction.

$$2NH_3 + CO_2 \rightarrow (NH_2)_2CO + H_2O$$

a) A company makes 120.6 tonnes of urea each day (where 1 tonne = 1 000 000 g). What mass of carbon dioxide is required to make this mass?

.... tonnes

[2]

b) Usually the reaction happens in an excess of ammonia. However, a leak in the reaction vessel means the mass of ammonia entering the reaction chamber each day is reduced to 59.5 tonnes.

What is the decrease, in tonnes, in the amount of urea produced per day?

.... tonnes

[3]

[Total 5 marks]

Topic C3 — Chemical Reactions

More Mole Calculations

1 An unknown hydrocarbon, **A**, completely combusts in oxygen to produce just water and carbon dioxide.

a) Given that four moles of carbon dioxide and four moles of water are produced during the combustion of 1 mole of **A**, suggest the chemical formula of hydrocarbon **A**.

....

[2]

b) Write a balanced chemical equation for the complete combustion of **A**.

....

[1]

[Total 3 marks]

2 Viola reacts an element, **X**, with oxygen. The result of the reaction is a single product, an oxide of element **X**.

a) Given that 200 g of **X** burn to produce 280 g of X oxide, what mass of oxygen gas was used in the reaction?

.... g

[1]

b) Given that the relative atomic mass of **X** is 40, write a balanced equation for the reaction of **X** with oxygen in the air. You should represent **X** oxide as X_aO_b, where a and b are integers.

....

[4]

[Total 5 marks]

3 A student reacts an unknown acid, H_2X, with sodium hydroxide, NaOH.
A neutralisation reaction takes place.
The products are a salt and one other product, Y.

a) i) What is the chemical formula of Y?

....

[1]

ii) Write a balanced equation for this reaction.

....

[2]

b) The total mass of the reactants was 228.2 g and 156.2 g of the salt was produced.

i) Calculate the number of moles of Y produced.

.... moles

[2]

ii) What mass of sodium hydroxide was used during this reaction?

.... g

[2]

iii) Find the relative molecular mass of the unknown acid.

....

[3]

iv) The student knows the acid is either chromic acid, (H_2CrO_4), hydrogen sulfide (H_2S)
or sulfuric acid (H_2SO_4). Deduce which of these is the correct identity of acid H_2X.

....

[1]

[Total 11 marks]

Exam Practice Tip

If a question involves dealing with moles of unknown masses, you can bet your bottom dollar that you're
going to need to be able to use the equations that link moles, mass and relative formula/atomic masses with
ease. Writing out this formula triangle that links these variables before you start these sorts of calculation
questions is always a good idea — it will help you to see what you can work out from what you're given.

Topic C3 — Chemical Reactions

Endothermic and Exothermic Reactions

1 Which of the following energy changes could be the result of an exothermic reaction?

	Energy of products	Temperature of surroundings
A	Greater than reactants	Increases
B	Less than reactants	Increases
C	Greater than reactants	Decreases
D	Less than reactants	Decreases

Your answer ☐

[Total 1 mark]

2 The reaction between ethanoic acid and sodium carbonate is an endothermic reaction.

Sketch and label a reaction profile for this reaction on the axes below.

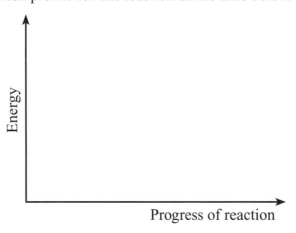

[Total 2 marks]

3 The diagram below shows the reaction profile for a chemical reaction.

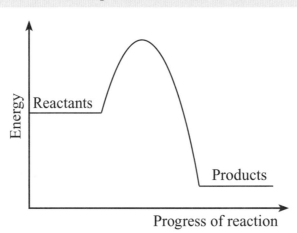

a) Mark the activation energy on the reaction profile.

[1]

b) Does this reaction profile show an endothermic or an exothermic reaction? Explain your answer.

....

....

[1]

[Total 2 marks]

Topic C3 — Chemical Reactions

Bond Energies

1   Which of the following statements is **true**?

     A   During exothermic reactions, the energy taken to break the bonds in the reactants is greater than the energy released by making the bonds in the products.

     B   During endothermic reactions, the energy released by breaking bonds in the reactants is less than the energy taken to make the bonds in the products.

     C   During exothermic reactions, the energy taken to break the bonds in the reactants is less than the energy released by making the bonds in the products.

     D   During endothermic reactions, the energy taken to break the bonds in the reactants is less than the energy released by making the bonds in the products.

Your answer ☐

[Total 1 mark]

2   Look at the table below. It shows the bond energies of some bonds. (Grade 6-7)

Bond	Bond energy (kJ/mol)
C — H	413
C — O	358
H — O	463
C = C	614
C — C	347

a)   Use the table to work out the energy change of the following reaction between ethene and water.

$$H_2C=CH_2 \ + \ H_2O \ \rightarrow \ H_3C-CH_2-O-H$$

.... kJ/mol

[3]

b)   Use your answer to a) to deduce whether the reaction between ethene and water is endothermic or exothermic. Explain your answer.

....

....

[2]

[Total 5 marks]

Topic C3 — Chemical Reactions

3   The energy change of the following reaction is –119 kJ/mol.

$$H-\underset{\underset{H}{|}}{\overset{\overset{H}{|}}{C}}-\underset{\underset{H}{|}}{\overset{\overset{H}{|}}{C}}-H \quad + \quad Cl-Cl \quad \rightarrow \quad H-\underset{\underset{H}{|}}{\overset{\overset{H}{|}}{C}}-\underset{\underset{H}{|}}{\overset{\overset{Cl}{|}}{C}}-H \quad + \quad H-Cl$$

a) Is the reaction endothermic or exothermic?

....

[1]

b) Use this information, as well as the data in the table,
   to work out the approximate bond energy of a H—Cl bond.

Bond	Bond energy (kJ/mol)
C — H	413
C — C	347
C — Cl	339
Cl — Cl	239

.... kJ/mol

[3]

c) Use your answer from b) to rank the bonds from the table,
   and the H—Cl bond in order of strength, from weakest to strongest.

....

[1]

[Total 5 marks]

Exam Practice Tip

In questions involving calculating energy changes from bond energies (or vice versa), it can be really useful to draw out the <u>displayed formulas</u> of any chemicals you're dealing with (unless you're given them in the question o' course). Displayed formulas show all the atoms and all the bonds between them, and make it easy to see what bonds have broken and what new bonds have been made during a chemical reaction.

Acids and Bases

1 Which of the following equations shows a neutralisation reaction?

    A $HNO_3 + LiOH \rightarrow LiNO_3 + H_2O$
    B $Mg + H_2O \rightarrow MgO + H_2$
    C $Na_2O + H_2O \rightarrow 2NaOH$
    D $C_4H_{10} + 6\frac{1}{2}O_2 \rightarrow 4CO_2 + 5H_2O$

Your answer ☐

[Total 1 mark]

2 Gemma and Srdjan are measuring the pHs of some common household substances using Universal indicator. **PRACTICAL**

a) They add a few drops of Universal indicator to some vinegar.
Given that vinegar is acidic, what colour would you expect the Universal indicator to turn?

....
[1]

b) They add a few drops of Universal indicator to a flask containing some kitchen cleaner.
A blue solution forms. Suggest a pH for the kitchen cleaner.

....
[1]

c) Gemma and Srdjan add Universal indicator to a sample of bleach. It produces a
purple colour. Gemma thinks it has a pH of 12 while Srdjan thinks it has a pH of 11.

Suggest an alternative piece of equipment they could use that
would give them a more accurate reading for the pH value.

....
[1]
[Total 3 marks]

3 Write an ionic equation to show the reaction of any acid and alkali.
Include state symbols.

....
[Total 2 marks]

Topic C3 — Chemical Reactions

4 Which one of the following statements about pH probes is **false**? (Grade 6-7) PRACTICAL

  A   pH probes give a numerical value for the pH of a solution.

  B   Before using a pH probe, you should calibrate it by
      setting it to measure pH 7 in a sample of pure water.

  C   You should wash a pH probe with a weak acid in between readings.

  D   pH probes measure pH electronically.

Your answer ☐

[Total 1 mark]

5 Pedro carries out an acid-base titration by adding a base to an acid. He measures the pH of the solution throughout the experiment, and uses the results to draw the titration curve, shown on the right. (Grade 7-9)

pH vs Volume of base added (cm^3) graph showing a titration curve rising from pH 1 to pH 13.

a) What was the starting pH of the acid?

....
[1]

b) Mark, with an asterisk (*), the end point of the titration on the curve on the graph.
[1]

c) How much base was needed to completely neutralise the volume of acid used in the titration?

.... cm^3
[1]

d) At the end point, how does the concentration of **hydrogen** ions
   compare with the concentration of **hydroxide** ions?

....
[1]

[Total 4 marks]

Strong and Weak Acids

1 Methanoic acid, HCOOH, is a **weak acid**. (Grade 6-7)

a) Explain what is meant by the term 'weak acid'.

....

....

[1]

b) Write a chemical equation to show how methanoic acid acts as a weak acid.

....

[2]

[Total 3 marks]

2 Tamal has two beakers, each containing a sample of a different acid.
The acid in beaker X is **stronger** than the acid in beaker Y.
The acid in beaker Y is **more concentrated** than the acid in beaker X. (Grade 6-7)

Which of the following options could describe the contents of the two beakers?

	Beaker X	Beaker Y
A	0.002 mol/dm³ HCl	4.0 mol/dm³ CH₃COOH
B	4.0 mol/dm³ HCl	0.002 mol/dm³ CH₃COOH
C	0.002 mol/dm³ CH₃COOH	4.0 mol/dm³ HCl
D	4.0 mol/dm³ CH₃COOH	0.002 mol/dm³ HCl

Your answer ☐

[Total 1 mark]

3 Jackie is carrying out an experiment to measure how the pH of a strong acid is affected by its concentration. (Grade 7-9)

a) Jackie takes a sample of an acidic solution, A, made by dissolving a solid acid in deionised water.
He wants to make his sample of the acid more concentrated.
Which of the following things could he do?

A Add a more dilute solution of the acid to the sample.
B Add more water to the sample.
C Add more solution the same as A to the sample.
D Dissolve more solid acid in the sample.

Your answer ☐

[1]

b) At a certain dilution, the hydrogen ion concentration is 0.001 mol/dm³ and the acid has a pH of 3.
Jackie increases the concentration of hydrogen ions in the sample to 0.1 mol/dm³.
What is the new pH of the acid?

....

[1]

[Total 2 marks]

Topic C3 — Chemical Reactions

Reactions of Acids

1   June allows a metal carbonate and an acid to react together in a flask.   *Grade 4-6*
    Which of the following chemicals are not produced?

    A   carbon dioxide
    B   a salt
    C   water
    D   hydrogen

    Your answer [ ]

    [Total 1 mark]

2   Complete the table to show the chemical formulas of the   *Grade 6-7*
    salts created in the reactions involving the following acids.

	Hydrochloric acid (HCl)	Nitric acid (HNO_3)	Sulfuric acid (H_2SO_4)
Zinc metal (Zn)	$ZnCl_2$	....	$ZnSO_4$
Calcium carbonate ($CaCO_3$)	$CaCl_2$	$Ca(NO_3)_2$	....
Sodium hydroxide (NaOH)	NaCl	$NaNO_3$	....
Potassium carbonate (K_2CO_3)	....	KNO_3	K_2SO_4

[Total 4 marks]

3   Andy is making a sample of potassium sulfate, K_2SO_4, by reacting   *Grade 6-7*   **PRACTICAL**
    potassium hydroxide, KOH, and sulfuric acid, H_2SO_4, together.

a) Potassium sulfate is a soluble salt. Explain what is meant by the term soluble in this context.

    ....
    [1]

b) Write a balanced chemical equation for this reaction.

    ....
    [2]

c) Andy uses a titration method to add a potassium hydroxide solution to the acid until he reaches the
    end point, which is shown by a change in colour of an indicator in the solution. He then crystallises
    the solution to obtain the salt. Will this produce a pure sample of the salt? Explain your answer.

    ....

    ....
    [1]

    [Total 4 marks]

Topic C3 — Chemical Reactions

4 Pauline mixes zinc carbonate, $ZnCO_3$, with hydrochloric acid, HCl, and notes that the mixture starts to bubble as a gas is given off. *Grade 6-7*

a) What is the name of the gas that is responsible for the bubbles in the reaction?

....

[1]

b) Write a balanced chemical equation for the reaction between hydrochloric acid and zinc carbonate.

....

[2]

c) What is the name of the salt produced by the reaction?

....

[1]

[Total 4 marks]

5 Sodium sulfate is a soluble salt that can be made by the reaction between sulfuric acid, H_2SO_4, and sodium hydroxide, NaOH solution. *Grade 7-9*

a) Write a balanced chemical equation for the reaction between sulfuric acid and sodium hydroxide.

....

[2]

b)* Outline how you could prepare a pure sample of sodium sulfate in the lab from sulfuric acid and sodium hydroxide. **PRACTICAL**

....

....

....

....

....

....

....

....

....

[6]

[Total 8 marks]

Exam Practice Tip

If you're asked to predict what will form in a reaction involving an acid, it can help to write out a balanced chemical equation. That way, you can see exactly what atoms you're dealing with in the reactants, and make sure they're all accounted for in the products. It may sound like a bit of an effort, but it will make sure you don't miss out anything.

Topic C3 — Chemical Reactions

Making Salts

1 Insoluble salts can be made by precipitation reactions.
Which of the following equations describes a precipitation reaction?

    A $CuO_{(s)} + 2HCl_{(aq)} \rightarrow CuCl_{2\ (aq)} + H_2O_{(l)}$

    B $HCl_{(aq)} + NaOH_{(aq)} \rightarrow NaCl_{(aq)} + H_2O_{(l)}$

    C $2HNO_{3\ (aq)} + ZnCO_{3\ (s)} \rightarrow Zn(NO_3)_{2\ (aq)} + H_2O_{(l)} + CO_{2\ (g)}$

    D $Pb(NO_3)_{2\ (aq)} + 2NaCl_{(aq)} \rightarrow PbCl_{2\ (s)} + 2NaNO_{3\ (aq)}$

    Your answer ☐

[Total 1 mark]

2 Jeremy is making a sample of silver chloride,
an insoluble salt, using an acid and a salt solution.

a) Suggest an acid that Jeremy could use to make silver chloride.

....

[1]

b) Once Jeremy has made the salt, he pours the whole
solid and salt solution into a filter funnel, as shown below.

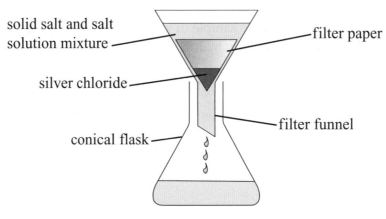

What has Jeremy done wrong? Explain how this will affect
the mass of solid salt that he collects from the solution.

....

....

....

[2]

c) After Jeremy has isolated the salt, he washes it with deionised water.
Explain why he uses deionised water as opposed to tap water.

....

....

[1]

[Total 4 marks]

3 The following steps describe how you would produce a pure sample of magnesium sulfate, $MgSO_4$, from solid magnesium hydroxide and sulfuric acid.

Grade 6-7

    1 Slowly heat the solution to evaporate off some of the water.

    2 Filter the solid off and dry it in a desiccator.

    3 Filter out the excess solid using a filter funnel and filter paper.

    4 Add magnesium hydroxide to a flask containing sulfuric acid until no more of the metal hydroxide reacts (at this point, the excess solid will just sink to the bottom of the flask).

    5 Leave the solution to crystallise.

a) Which is the correct order that these steps should be carried out in?

    A   4, 1, 3, 2, 5

    B   1, 4, 2, 5, 2

    C   4, 3, 1, 5, 2

    D   3, 1, 2, 5, 4

Your answer ☐

[1]

b) Write a balanced symbol equation, including state symbols, that describes the reaction between magnesium hydroxide, $Mg(OH)_2$, and sulfuric acid, H_2SO_4.

....

[3]

[Total 4 marks]

4 Davina reacts iron nitrate, $Fe(NO_3)_3$, and sodium hydroxide, NaOH, together to make an insoluble salt containing iron.

Grade 6-7

a) Write down the chemical formula of the insoluble salt.

....

[1]

b) The following steps outline the method Davina used to make the insoluble salt.

> **1.** Mix equal quantities of iron nitrate and sodium hydroxide.
>
> **2.** Once a precipitate has started to form, filter the solution to remove the solid.
>
> **3.** Heat the solid with a Bunsen burner to dry it.

Suggest **two** improvements that you could make to Davina's method to ensure that all the insoluble salt is extracted and that the final sample is pure.

....

....

....

....

[2]

[Total 3 marks]

Oxidation and Reduction

1 The combustion of hydrocarbons can be described as an oxidation reaction. Explain why. **Grade 4-6**

....

....

[Total 1 mark]

2 Which of the following statements is **false**? **Grade 4-6**

    A   Oxidation is the gain of oxygen.

    B   Reduction and oxidation happen at the same time.

    C   Reduction is the loss of electrons.

    D   Reducing agents donate electrons.

Your answer ☐

[Total 1 mark]

3 In a redox reaction, aluminium atoms are oxidised to Al^{3+} ions. **Grade 6-7**

a) Write a balanced half equation to show this reaction. Use e^- to represent an electron.

....

[1]

b) In the redox reaction, would aluminium act as an oxidising agent or a reducing agent?

....

[1]

[Total 2 marks]

4 The following ionic equation shows a redox reaction involving hydrogen ions and zinc. **Grade 7-9**

$$Zn + 2H^+ \rightarrow Zn^{2+} + H_2$$

a) Write balanced half equations to show how electrons are transferred in this reaction.
Use e^- to represent an electron.

    i) Zinc half equation: ....

[1]

    ii) Hydrogen half equation:..

[1]

b) What is the oxidising agent in the reaction?

....

[1]

c) Which element was oxidised in the reaction?

....

[1]

[Total 4 marks]

Topic C3 — Chemical Reactions

Electrolysis

Fill in the labels on the diagram, using the words below, to show the different parts of the electrochemical cell.

wires   cathode   electrolyte   power supply   anode

1   As part of an industrial process, a sample of sodium chloride, NaCl, was electrolysed. **Grade 4-6**

a) Before the sodium chloride is electrolysed, it either has to be molten or dissolved in solution. Explain why this is necessary.

....

....

[2]

b) Given that inert electrodes were used and the sodium chloride was molten, what would be formed at:

i) the anode? ....

[1]

ii) the cathode? ....

[1]

[Total 4 marks]

2   The two half equations below show the reactions happening at the anode and the cathode during an electrolysis experiment.

$$Pb^{2+} + 2e^- \rightarrow Pb$$
$$2I^- \rightarrow I_2 + 2e^-$$

a) Give the chemical formula of the electrolyte, given that it's a molten metal compound.

....

[1]

b) What would you expect to happen at the cathode?

....

[1]

[Total 2 marks]

3 Zoe sets up an electrochemical cell. A diagram of her set up is shown below.

Grade 6-7

PRACTICAL

wires

beaker

inert electrodes

electrolyte

What **two** things are wrong with Zoe's set-up?

....

....

[Total 2 marks]

4 Matthew carries out an electrolysis experiment using inert electrodes. The electrolyte he uses is a solution of potassium nitrate.

Grade 6-7

a) Matthew predicts that potassium will be discharged at the cathode. Given that potassium is more reactive than hydrogen, do you agree with Matthew? Explain your answer.

....

....

[2]

b) Describe what you would expect to see happening at the anode. Explain your answer.

....

....

[2]

[Total 4 marks]

5 Electrolysis is carried out on a solution of copper(II) chloride, $CuCl_2$, using inert electrodes.

Grade 6-7

a) Which of the following ions is **not** present in the solution?

A H^+
B H_2O^-
C Cu^{2+}
D Cl^-

Your answer ☐

[1]

b) What would you expect to see happen at:

i) the anode? ....

ii) the cathode? ....

[2]

[Total 3 marks]

Electrolysis of Copper Sulfate

1 The following question is about the electrolysis of copper sulfate solution using platinum electrodes.

Grade 6-7

PRACTICAL

a) Platinum electrodes are an example of an inert electrode.
Explain what is meant, in this context, by the term 'inert'.

....
[1]

b) Assuming the copper sulfate is pure, list the four ions that are present in solution during the electrolysis of copper sulfate solution using inert electrodes.

....
[2]

c) Write balanced half equations to show the reactions that occur at:

i) the anode ....

ii) the cathode ....
[2]
[Total 5 marks]

2 Lucy has two identical strips of copper. She uses them as electrodes in the electrochemical cell shown on the right.

Grade 6-7

a) She places the electrochemical cell on a mass balance and turns on the power supply. She leaves the power supply on for 30 minutes, and monitors the mass of the cell throughout the reaction. How would you expect the mass of the cell to change over the 30 minutes?

....
[1]

b) After 30 minutes, Lucy turns the power supply off and disconnects the electrodes. How would you expect the appearances of each electrode to have changed throughout the electrolysis? Explain your answer.

....

....

....

....
[3]
[Total 4 marks]

52

3 Which of the following statements best describes what occurs during the electrolysis of copper sulfate with copper electrodes?

    A   Copper atoms are transferred from the cathode to the anode.
    B   Sulfate ions are discharged at the anode.
    C   Copper atoms are oxidised to Cu^{3+} ions.
    D   Copper ions are reduced to copper atoms at the cathode.

Your answer ☐

[Total 1 mark]

4 Valentino is investigating the electrolysis of copper sulfate. He sets up two cells. In cell A he uses platinum electrodes. In cell B, he uses copper electrodes. The cells are identical in all other respects.

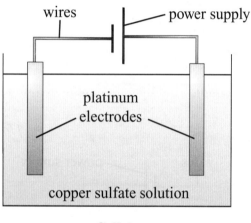
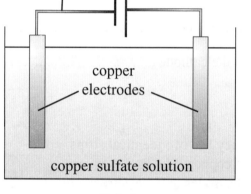

                   Cell A   **Cell B**

Both cells are turned on and left for 5 hours. Given that the masses of the two cells were the same at the start of the electrolysis, how would you expect them to compare after the 5 hours? Explain your answer. Use appropriate half equations to justify your answer.

....

....

....

....

....

....

....

[Total 5 marks]

Exam Practice Tip

When dealing with electrolysis questions (like the ones on the last four pages), read the question carefully, and then read it again. The products of electrolysis depends on loads of things — whether your electrolyte is molten or aqueous, what your electrodes are made of and what ions are present in your electrolyte. So, make sure you know exactly what set-up you're dealing with before you jump in with an answer. You have been warned...

Topic C3 — Chemical Reactions   ☐ ☐ ☐

Group 1 — Alkali Metals

1 The Group 1 elements are metals with relatively low melting and boiling points. They react readily to form ionic compounds. Their ions usually have a charge of 1+.

Grade 6-7

a) Explain why the elements in Group 1 usually form 1+ ions.

....

....

[2]

b) The table below shows information about the melting and boiling points of the first three Group 1 elements.

Element	Melting point (°C)	Boiling point (°C)
Lithium	181	1342
Sodium	....	883
Potassium	63	759

Use the information in the table to predict the melting point of sodium. Put your answer in the table.

[1]

[Total 3 marks]

PRACTICAL

2 A teacher adds a small piece of sodium to cold water. The sodium floats around on the surface, fizzing fairly vigorously, and melts as it reacts.

Grade 6-7

a) Name the **two** products of this reaction.

....

[2]

b) Describe what you would expect to see if a small piece of potassium was added to cold water.

....

....

....

....

[4]

c) It is safe to demonstrate the reaction between potassium and water in a school laboratory, but it is **not** safe to demonstrate the reaction between rubidium and water. Explain why.

....

....

[1]

[Total 7 marks]

Group 7 — Halogens

The sentences below are about the elements in Group 7 of the periodic table.
Choose from the words on the right to fill the gaps. Use each word only once.

The five known Group 7 elements, or halogens, are fluorine, chlorine, bromine,

.... and astatine. They have similar chemical properties, because

they all have .... electrons in their outer shell. The halogens

exist as .... molecules, where two halogen atoms share a pair of

electrons in a .... bond. A halogen atom can also form a stable

ion by gaining one electron — these ions are called .... ions.

diatomic

seven

halide

iodine

covalent

---

1 The melting and boiling points of the halogens **increase** as you move down Group 7. *Grade 4-6*

a) State which element in Group 7 will have the **lowest** boiling point.

....
[1]

b) At room temperature and pressure, chlorine is a gas, bromine is a liquid and iodine is a solid.
Use this information to predict the physical state of the element astatine at room temperature.

....
[1]

[Total 2 marks]

---

2 The halogens can react with alkali metals to form metal halide salts. *Grade 6-7*

a) Name the metal halide salt that will be formed when the following pairs of elements react.

i) Bromine and sodium.

....
[1]

ii) Iodine and potassium.

....
[1]

b) When chlorine gas reacts with lithium, the salt lithium chloride, LiCl, is formed.
Construct the balanced symbol equation for this reaction.

....
[2]

[Total 4 marks]

Topic 4 — Predicting and Identifying Reactions and Products

PRACTICAL

3 Josie investigated the reactions that occur when chlorine, bromine or iodine are added to different sodium halide solutions. The table below shows her results.

	Sodium chloride solution (NaCl $_{(aq)}$, colourless)	Sodium bromide solution (NaBr $_{(aq)}$, colourless)	Sodium iodide solution (NaI $_{(aq)}$, colourless)
Add chlorine water (Cl$_{2\,(aq)}$, colourless)	no reaction	solution turns orange	solution turns brown
Add bromine water (Br$_{2\,(aq)}$, orange)	no reaction	....	solution turns brown
Add iodine water (I$_{2\,(aq)}$, brown)	no reaction	no reaction	no reaction

a) Use your knowledge of the reactivity trend of the halogens to fill in the missing result in the table.

[1]

b) Explain why there was no reaction when Josie added iodine water to sodium bromide solution.

....

....

[2]

c) Construct a balanced symbol equation for the reaction that happened when Josie added chlorine water to sodium bromide solution.

....

[2]

[Total 5 marks]

4 There is a trend in the reactivity of the Group 7 elements.

a) State the trend in reactivity as you go down Group 7.

....

[1]

b) Explain the trend you have described in part a). Give your answer in terms of electronic structure.

....

....

....

....

[3]

[Total 4 marks]

   Topic 4 — Predicting and Identifying Reactions and Products

Group 0 — Noble Gases

1   Which of these statements is **true** for the noble gases?   Grade 4-6

    A   They are colourful gases.
    B   They have only 1 electron in their outer shells.
    C   They are monatomic.
    D   They react with alkali metals to form salts.

Your answer ☐

[Total 1 mark]

2   The noble gases are inert gases that make up Group 0 of the periodic table.   Grade 6-7

a) 'Inert' means 'very unreactive'. Explain why the elements in Group 0 are inert.

....

....

....

[2]

b) The table below shows some information about the first four noble gases.

Element	Symbol	Melting point (°C)	Boiling point (°C)	Density (kg/m³)
Helium	He	−272	−269	0.2
Neon	Ne	−249	−246	0.9
Argon	Ar	−189	−186	1.8
Krypton	Kr	−157	−153	3.7

i) The element below krypton in Group 0 is xenon.
   Use the information in the table to predict what the density of xenon will be.

....

[1]

ii) Would you expect the melting point of xenon to be higher or lower
   than the melting point of krypton? Explain your answer.

....

....

[1]

[Total 4 marks]

Exam Practice Tip

Make sure you get lots of practice at questions like 2 b), where you're given information about some of the elements in a group and asked to use it to predict something about another element in the group — they need careful thinking through. Remember, you could get asked to do this sort of thing for elements in Group 1, Group 7 or Group 0.

Topic 4 — Predicting and Identifying Reactions and Products

Transition Metals

Warm-Up

The statement below is about the position of the transition metals in the periodic table.
Cross out the incorrect words from the box to complete the sentence.

The transition metals can be found

| on the left / in the middle / on the right |

of the periodic table.

Circle all of the elements listed below that are transition metals.
(Use a periodic table to help with this bit if you need it.)

nickel   sulfur   chromium   tin

magnesium

calcium   aluminium   silver   iodine

potassium   titanium   cobalt   silicon

---

1   Transition metals and their compounds have many different uses.
Four examples of the uses of transition metals and their compounds,
are listed below. For each example, give **one** common property of
the transition metals that makes the material suitable for that use.

Grade
4-6

a) Gold can be used to make connectors and contacts in electrical circuits.

....
[1]

b) Tungsten can be used to make heating elements in furnaces.

....
[1]

c) Oxides of iron can be used to make stained glass for windows.

....
[1]

d) Copper can be used to make pipes to carry water.

....
[1]

[Total 4 marks]

2 Vanadium is a transition metal with atomic number 23.
Several different oxides of vanadium exist, for example VO_2 and V_2O_5.

Grade 6-7

a) What property of the transition metals means that it is possible
for vanadium to form both VO_2 and V_2O_5?

....

[1]

b) Vanadium pentoxide, V_2O_5, is added to the reaction vessel during the Contact Process,
which is used to produce sulfuric acid from sulfur, oxygen and water.
Suggest what role vanadium pentoxide is playing in this process.

....

[1]

c) Carys has samples of vanadium(IV) oxide, VO_2, and sodium oxide, Na_2O.
One is a deep blue powder and the other is a white powder.
Which one would you expect to be the vanadium(IV) oxide? Explain your answer.

....

....

[1]

[Total 3 marks]

PRACTICAL

3 Darren is given samples of four mystery metals, labelled **A**, **B**, **C** and **D**.
He performs several tests on the samples to investigate their properties.

Grade 6-7

a) Darren heats metals **A** and **B** using a Bunsen burner. Metal **A** melts quickly, but metal **B** does not
melt. State which of the two metals is more likely to be a transition metal. Explain your answer.

....

....

[1]

b) The diagram below shows what happened when Darren
placed small pieces of metals **C** and **D** into cold water.

State which of the two metals is more likely to be a transition metal.
Give **two** observations from the diagram that support your answer.

....

....

....

....

[2]

[Total 3 marks]

Topic 4 — Predicting and Identifying Reactions and Products

Reactivity of Metals

1 Amal performed some experiments to investigate the reactivity of metals.

a) First, Amal placed pieces of four different metals into dilute hydrochloric acid.
The diagram below shows what the four experiments looked like after 1 minute.

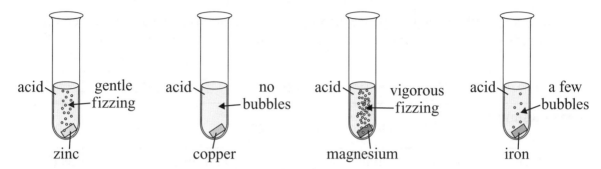

Use the information in the diagram to put these metals in order of reactivity.

Most reactive: ....

....

....

Least reactive: ....

[2]

b) Next, Amal was given samples of three mystery metals, marked **X**, **Y** and **Z**. She put small
pieces of each of the metals in cold water. If there was no reaction with cold water, she
tested the metal to see if it would react with steam. Her results are shown in the table below.

Metal	Any reaction with cold water?	Any reaction with steam?
X	Reacts vigorously. Hydrogen gas is produced.	
Y	no reaction	Reacts vigorously. Metal is coated with a white solid. Hydrogen gas is produced.
Z	no reaction	no reaction

i) Metal **Y** was zinc. It reacted with the steam to produce hydrogen gas and a white solid.
Name the white solid that was produced by this reaction.

....

[1]

ii) One of the other metals Amal was given was sodium.
Suggest whether sodium was metal **X** or metal **Z**. Give a reason for your answer.

....

....

[1]

[Total 4 marks]

Topic 4 — Predicting and Identifying Reactions and Products

60

2   Which of the statements below about metal reactivity is **incorrect**?    **PRACTICAL**

   A   The easier it is for a metal atom to form a positive ion, the less reactive it will be.
   B   A metal will displace a less reactive metal from a salt solution.
   C   In a reactivity series, you will find a reactive metal above a less reactive metal.
   D   The more reactive a metal is, the faster its reaction with dilute acid will be.

   Your answer [   ]   *[Total 1 mark]*

3   Shaun adds small pieces of some metals to metal salt solutions and leaves them for 1 hour. Grade 7-9
     He records whether or not any reaction has taken place. His table of results is shown below.

	Magnesium	**Silver**	**Aluminium**	**Lead**
Magnesium chloride	no reaction	no reaction	no reaction	no reaction
Silver nitrate	magnesium nitrate and silver formed	no reaction	aluminium nitrate and silver formed	lead nitrate and silver formed
Aluminium chloride	magnesium chloride and aluminium formed	no reaction	no reaction	no reaction
Lead nitrate	magnesium nitrate and lead formed	no reaction	aluminium nitrate and lead formed	no reaction

a) Shaun says "My results show that lead is more reactive than silver."
   Do you agree? Explain your answer.

   ....

   ....
                                                                                   [1]

b) Construct a balanced symbol equation for the reaction between magnesium
   and aluminium chloride, $AlCl_3$.

   ....
                                                                                   [2]

c) Nickel is above lead in the reactivity series. Nickel is a shiny grey metal and nickel nitrate
   is green in solution. Lead is a dull grey metal and lead nitrate is colourless in solution.
   Suggest what Shaun would observe if he added nickel to lead nitrate solution.

   ....

   ....

   ....
                                                                                   [2]
                                                                         [Total 5 marks]

Exam Practice Tip

It sounds a bit obvious, but the main thing to remember when you're answering questions on this topic is that the more
reactive a metal is, the more likely it will be to react and form a compound. So the more reactive a metal is, the more
vigorously it will react with water and acids, and a reactive metal will push a less reactive metal out of a salt solution...

Topic 4 — Predicting and Identifying Reactions and Products

Tests for Gases

1 Amelia is testing for gases.

The diagram below shows a gas being tested.

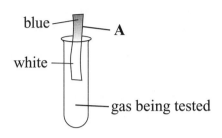

a) Identify the item labelled **A** in the diagram.

....
[1]

b Suggest which gas was present in the test tube.

....
[1]
[Total 2 marks]

2 Vicky performs an experiment that produces a colourless gas. Vicky does not know what the gas is, so she collects it and tests it in order to identify it. Grade 6-7

a) Suggest why Vicky should perform the experiment in a fume cupboard.

....
[1]

b) Describe how Vicky could test the gas to see if it was carbon dioxide.

....

....
[2]

c) When Vicky placed a lighted splint into a sample of the gas, it was **not** accompanied by a popping sound. What does this tell you about the gas she had collected?

....
[1]

d) When Vicky placed a glowing splint into a sample of the gas, the splint relighted. Identify the gas that was produced by her experiment.

....
[1]
[Total 5 marks]

     Topic 4 — Predicting and Identifying Reactions and Products

Tests for Ions

1 Kelly has a small bottle of a clear solution labelled "calcium sulfate solution". Her teacher asks her to perform some tests to confirm that the bottle of solution has been correctly labelled.

a) First Kelly tests the solution for calcium ions using the method shown in the box below. The name of the solution she used in step 1 has been replaced with 'Solution **A**'.

> Method for testing for calcium ions
> 1. Clean a nichrome wire loop by dipping it into Solution A.
> 2. Rinse the loop in deionised water.
> 3. Dip the wire loop into the test solution.
> 4. Put the wire loop in the clear part of a Bunsen flame.
> 5. Record the colour of the flame.

i) Suggest what Solution **A** is.

....

[1]

ii) Name the colour of the flame that will be produced if the solution being tested does contain calcium ions.

....

[1]

b) Next, Kelly tests the solution for sulfate ions using the method shown in the box below.

> Method for testing for sulfate ions
> 1. Place 3 cm^3 of your test solution in a test tube.
> 2. Add 10 drops of barium chloride solution.
> 3. If a precipitate has formed, add 3 cm^3 of hydrochloric acid to the test tube and observe what happens.

Kelly's test solution does contain sulfate ions.
When she adds barium chloride to the test solution in step 2, a white precipitate forms.

i) Name the compound that the white precipitate is made up of.

....

[1]

ii) Predict what will happen when Kelly adds hydrochloric acid to the precipitate in step 3. Explain your answer.

....

....

[2]

[Total 5 marks]

2 Various tests can be used to identify which metal ion is present in a compound. Grade 4-6

a) Suggest what metal ion is present in a compound that burns with a crimson flame in a flame test.

....
[1]

b) Copper(II) nitrate is a soluble salt that contains copper(II) ions.

i) What colour flame would you expect this compound to burn with in a flame test?

....
[1]

ii) If you dissolved this compound in water and then added a few drops of sodium hydroxide, what would you expect to observe?

....
[1]

[Total 3 marks]

3 Mark is given samples of three solutions, **A**, **B**, and **C**. He tests each of them with acidified silver nitrate solution and sodium hydroxide solution. His table of results is shown below. Grade 6-7

Test	Solution A	Solution B	Solution C
Add acidified silver nitrate solution	yellow precipitate forms	no reaction	yellow precipitate forms
Add a few drops of sodium hydroxide solution	white precipitate forms	brown precipitate forms	green precipitate forms

a) Suggest which metal ion solution **B** contains.

....
[1]

b) Suggest the formula of the compound in solution **C**.

....
[1]

c) i) Mark says "I can tell from my results that solution **A** contains zinc ions."
Explain why Mark is wrong.

....

....
[1]

ii) If solution **A** did contain zinc ions, what would you expect Mark to observe if he added more NaOH to the test tube?

....
[1]

[Total 4 marks]

Topic 4 — Predicting and Identifying Reactions and Products

64

4 The compound potassium sodium carbonate has the formula $KNaCO_3$. (Grade 6-7)

a) Explain why it would be difficult to identify the positive ions in this compound using a flame test.

....

....

[1]

b) Describe how you could test a solution of this compound to show that it contained carbonate ions.

....

....

....

....

....

....

[5]

[Total 6 marks]

5* Oliver was asked to prepare a sample of potassium chloride. He designed a suitable method and carried it out. When he had finished, he had 5 g of the solid salt. Describe how Oliver could show that the salt he has made is potassium chloride. In your answer you should give the methods for any tests that you suggest. (Grade 7-9)

....

....

....

....

....

....

....

....

....

....

....

....

[Total 6 marks]

Topic 4 — Predicting and Identifying Reactions and Products

Chemical Analysis

1 Give **three** advantages of using instrumental methods to analyse a substance, rather than analysing it by hand.

Grade 4-6

1. ....

....

2. ....

....

3. ....

....

[Total 3 marks]

2 A scientist used gas chromatography to analyse a mixture of compounds. The chromatogram produced by the mixture is shown on the right. Each compound in the mixture produced one peak on the chromatogram.

Grade 6-7

a) State how many different compounds there were in the mixture.

....

[1]

b) The scientist used the same machine to analyse samples of pure propene, propanol, butene and butanol. The chromatograms for these experiments are shown below.

Which of these four compounds do these results suggest were present in the mixture?

....

[2]

[Total 3 marks]

3   Infrared spectroscopy is a method of chemical analysis. It produces a graph, called
a spectrum, which has peaks representing the different types of bond present in each
molecule of a compound. The table below shows the frequencies of the infrared
spectrum peaks that correspond to certain common bonds.

Bond	Frequency / Wavenumber (cm^{-1})
C–C	750 - 1100
C–O	1000 - 1300
C=C	1620 - 1680
O–H (in a carboxylic acid)	2500 - 3000
C–H	2850 - 3300
O–H (in an alcohol)	3230 - 3550

A scientist used infrared spectroscopy to analyse a compound.
This table shows the frequencies of the four main peaks (**A** to **D**) on the scientist's spectrum:

Peak	Frequency / Wavenumber (cm^{-1})
A	900
B	1150
C	3100
D	3400

a) Use the data tables to identify which type of bond caused each peak on the scientist's spectrum.

Peak **A**: ....   Peak **B**: ....

Peak **C**: ....   Peak **D**: ....

[2]

b) Anna says that she thinks that the molecule
the scientist was analysing was propene.
The displayed formula of propene is shown on the right.

Propene does not produce the infrared spectrum that the scientist saw, so Anna is **incorrect**.
State **two** ways in which the propene molecule does not match up with the scientist's spectrum.

1. ....

....

2. ....

....

[2]

[Total 4 marks]

Exam Practice Tip

Apart from giving the advantages of instrumental methods, the main thing you need to be able to do for this topic is
to interpret data (like tables and graphs) that shows the results of using an instrumental method. So don't panic if a
question involves a technique that you don't recognise — all the information you need will be there in the question.

Topic 4 — Predicting and Identifying Reactions and Products

Concentration

Warm-Up

Circle the formula triangle below which is **correct**.

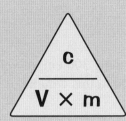 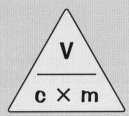 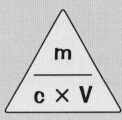

m = mass
c = concentration
V = Volume

1 A student makes a saline solution by dissolving 36 g of sodium chloride in 0.40 dm³ of water. What is the concentration of the solution?

- **A** 90 g/dm³
- **B** 14.4 g/dm³
- **C** 14 400 g/dm³
- **D** 0.090 g/dm³

Your answer ☐

[Total 1 mark]

2 A student makes up a volume of a standard solution of copper sulfate, **X**, with a concentration of 75.0 g/dm³. He does this by dissolving copper sulfate in 220 cm³ of water.

a) Calculate the mass of copper sulfate that was used to make the solution.

Mass = ... g

[1]

b) Calculate the concentration of the standard solution, **X**, in mol/dm³.
Give your answer to 2 significant figures. Relative formula mass (M_r): $CuSO_4$ = 159.6

Concentration = ... mol/dm³

[1]

c) Which of the following statements is **true**?

- **A** **X** will become more concentrated if more water is added to the solution.
- **B** Dissolving 56 g of copper sulfate in 220 cm³ of water will make a solution more concentrated than **X**.
- **C** Adding an additional 10 g of the solute to **X** will make the solution less concentrated.
- **D** The concentration of **X** will halve if an additional 10 cm³ of water are added to the solution.

Your answer ☐

[1]

[Total 3 marks]

3 A student dissolves 56 g of potassium chloride in 400 cm³ of water. *Grade* **6-7**

a) Calculate the concentration of the resultant potassium chloride solution in g/dm³.

Concentration = ... g/dm³
[1]

b) The student wants to make a solution with the same concentration using only 300 cm³ of water. Calculate the mass of potassium chloride that the student will need to add to this volume of water.

Mass = ... g
[1]

[Total 2 marks]

4 A lab technician is making up some solutions for students to use in some of their classes. *Grade* **7-9**

a) The technician makes a standard solution of sodium hydroxide for a titration experiment. She makes 600 cm³ of the solution at a concentration of 5.00 mol/dm³.

Calculate the mass of sodium hydroxide used to make the solution.
Give your answer to 3 significant figures. Relative formula mass (M_r): NaOH = 40.0

Mass = ... g
[2]

b) i) The technician also makes a standard solution of sodium carbonate. The solution has a concentration of 80.0 g/dm³ and was made by adding 36.0 g of sodium carbonate to a volume of water. Calculate the volume of water, in cm³, that she used to make the solution.

Volume of water = ... cm³
[2]

ii) For a separate experiment, the technician needs a sodium carbonate solution with a concentration of 40.0 g/dm³.
What can she do to her 80.0 g/dm³ solution to make it this concentration?

....
[1]

[Total 5 marks]

Exam Practice Tip

Make sure you pay close attention to the units used in the question. You might need to convert some values before you can carry out any calculations, e.g. converting volumes from cm³ to dm³ by dividing by 1000. You might also need to convert some values at the end, e.g. if they ask for the concentration of the solution in mol/dm³ instead of in g/dm³.

Topic C5 — Monitoring and Controlling Chemical Reactions

Titrations

1   A student carried out a titration where 0.165 mol/dm³ hydrochloric acid was used to neutralise 22.0 cm³ of magnesium hydroxide solution. He repeated the titration three times.

a) Calculate the mean titre of hydrochloric acid using the results in the table below.
Ignore any anomalous results.

	Titration			
	1	2	3	4
Titre (cm³)	35.10	33.30	33.40	33.35

Mean = ... cm³
[1]

b) Using your result from part a), calculate the number of moles of hydrochloric acid that were needed to neutralise the solution of magnesium hydroxide. Give your answer to 3 significant figures.

Moles = ... mol
[1]
[Total 2 marks]

2   Annalise carried out four repeats of a titration. She calculated the mean titre and found that 40.0 cm³ of 0.100 mol/dm³ sodium hydroxide was used to neutralise 20.0 cm³ of hydrochloric acid. The equation for the reaction is: NaOH + HCl → NaCl + H₂O

a) Calculate the concentration of the hydrochloric acid in mol/dm³.

Concentration = ... mol/dm³
[2]

b) Convert the concentration of the hydrochloric acid to g/dm³.

Concentration = ... g/dm³
[2]
[Total 4 marks]

Topic C5 — Monitoring and Controlling Chemical Reactions

3 A chemist completes a titration where 0.00850 mol of potassium hydroxide is neutralised by 0.0250 dm³ of sulfuric acid. The equation for the reaction is:

Grade
6-7

$$2KOH + H_2SO_4 \rightarrow K_2SO_4 + 2H_2O$$

What is the concentration of the sulfuric acid in g/dm³?
Relative formula mass (M_r): $H_2SO_4 = 98.1$

A   0.170 g/dm³
B   16.7 g/dm³
C   1.66 g/dm³
D   17.3 g/dm³

Your answer ☐

[Total 1 mark]

4 Amy has a sodium hydroxide solution of an unknown concentration. She also plans to find the concentration of the solution by titrating it with a 0.200 mol/dm³ standard solution of sulfuric acid.

Grade
7-9

PRACTICAL

a)* Describe how to carry out a titration, with reference to the equipment used.

....

....

....

....

....

....

....

....

....

....

[6]

b) It took 22.5 cm³ of the standard solution to neutralise 25.0 cm³ sodium hydroxide solution. Calculate the concentration of the sodium hydroxide. Give your answer to 3 significant figures. The equation for the reaction is: $2NaOH + H_2SO_4 \rightarrow Na_2SO_4 + 2H_2O$

Concentration = ... mol/dm³
[2]

[Total 8 marks]

Topic C5 — Monitoring and Controlling Chemical Reactions

Calculations with Gases

1 Chloé says that at room temperature and pressure, the volume of 23 moles of carbon dioxide is equal to the volume of 23 moles of oxygen. Kira says that the volume of the carbon dioxide will be greater because carbon dioxide has a greater relative formula mass.

a) Which student is correct? Explain your answer.

....

....

....

[2]

b) Calculate the volume of 23.0 moles of oxygen, O_2, at room temperature and pressure.

Volume = ... dm³

[1]

[Total 3 marks]

2 A student took some calcium carbonate, in the form of marble chips, and added hydrochloric acid. The equation for the reaction is:
$$CaCO_{3(s)} + 2HCl_{(aq)} \rightarrow CaCl_{2(aq)} + CO_{2(g)} + H_2O_{(l)}$$

a) 920 cm³ of carbon dioxide, CO_2, was produced during the reaction. This had a mass of 1.76 g. Calculate the molar volume of the carbon dioxide.

Molar volume = ... dm³/mol

[2]

b) The student repeated the experiment under a different set of conditions. This time, 175 cm³ of carbon dioxide with a molar volume of 25.0 dm³/mol was produced. Calculate the mass of carbon dioxide produced in this reaction.

Mass = ... g

[2]

[Total 4 marks]

   Topic C5 — Monitoring and Controlling Chemical Reactions

Percentage Yield

1 Kezia and Steven are reacting some lithium with water to form lithium hydroxide and hydrogen gas. From the mass of reactants, they calculate the theoretical yield of lithium hydroxide to be 25 g.

Grade 4-6

a) Kezia finds that 17 g of lithium hydroxide is produced.
What is the percentage yield of lithium hydroxide?

A   63%

B   72%

C   68%

D   54%

Your answer ☐

[1]

b) Steven's experiment produces 22 g of lithium hydroxide.
Calculate the percentage yield of lithium hydroxide in his reaction.

Percentage yield = ... %
[1]
[Total 2 marks]

2 In a precipitation reaction, copper sulfate solution reacts with sodium hydroxide solution. The equation for the reaction is:
$$CuSO_4 + 2NaOH \rightarrow Cu(OH)_2 + Na_2SO_4$$

Grade 6-7

a) If 39.75 g of copper sulfate reacts with an excess of sodium hydroxide, calculate the theoretical yield of the copper hydroxide. Give your answer to 3 significant figures.

Theoretical yield = ... g
[3]

b) A student carries out this reaction and produces 16.5 g of copper hydroxide. Use your answer in part a) to calculate the percentage yield of the reaction to 3 significant figures.

Percentage yield = ... %
[1]
[Total 4 marks]

3 Limestone is mainly composed of calcium carbonate.
When heated, it thermally decomposes to form calcium oxide and carbon dioxide.
The equation for the reaction is: $CaCO_3 \rightarrow CaO + CO_2$

Grade
7-9

a) In an industrial reaction, 68.00 kg of calcium carbonate decomposed to form
28.56 kg of calcium oxide, CaO. Calculate the percentage yield of calcium oxide.

Percentage yield = ... %

[4]

b) The 28.56 kg of calcium oxide produced from the above reaction was reacted with water
to form 32.80 kg of slaked lime, $Ca(OH)_2$, which is used in water and sewage treatment.
The equation for the reaction is: $CaO + H_2O \rightarrow Ca(OH)_2$
Calculate the percentage yield of slaked lime to 3 significant figures.

Percentage yield = ... %

[4]

c) Using your answers from a) and b), suggest which of the two reactions is the **most** economic?
Explain your answer.

....

....

....

[2]

[Total 10 marks]

Topic C5 — Monitoring and Controlling Chemical Reactions

Atom Economy

Warm-Up

Complete the table by calculating the atom economy for the two reactions.

Reaction	M_r of desired product	Total M_r of all products	Atom Economy (%)
NaOH + HCl → NaCl + H_2O	58.5	76.5	....
2Cu + O_2 → 2CuO	159	159	....

1   Some chemicals can be made by several different reactions. Industrial companies need to take different factors into consideration before deciding which reaction pathway is the most profitable and environmentally friendly. The table below shows data for three different reactions that each produce the same desired product.

Reaction	Atom Economy (%)	Percentage Yield (%)	Rate	Useful By-product
A	100	84	Medium	No
B		64	Slow	Yes
C	73.5	53	Fast	No

a) i) Give the definition of atom economy.

....

....
                                                                                                                                    [1]

ii) In reaction **B**, the relative formula mass of all the products is 141 and the relative formula mass of the desired product is 111. Use this data to calculate the atom economy of the reaction. Give your answer to 3 significant figures.

Atom economy = ... %
                                                                                                                                    [1]

b) Use the table and your answer to part a) ii) to determine which reaction pathway would be the most suitable to be carried out in industry. Explain your answer.

....

....

....

....

....
                                                                                                                                    [3]

[Total 5 marks]

2 Magnesium chloride has a variety of applications, including use in fertilisers, waste water treatment and medicine. It can be produced by several different reactions. Three reactions are shown below.

X $Mg + 2HCl \rightarrow MgCl_2 + H_2$

Y $MgCO_3 + 2HCl \rightarrow MgCl_2 + H_2O + CO_2$

Z $MgO + 2HCl \rightarrow MgCl_2 + H_2O$

a) Calculate the atom economy of each reaction. Give your answers to 2 significant figures.

X = ... %

Y = ... %

Z = ... %

[7]

b) A company is looking at the cost implications of using each of the reactions. Explain how the atom economy of a reaction can affect:

i) the amount of raw materials needed to make a certain amount of product.

....

....

[1]

ii) the cost associated with disposing of chemical waste.

....

....

[1]

c) Using your answers to part a), suggest which of the three reactions, **X**, **Y** or **Z**, would be the **least** profitable method for making magnesium chloride in industry.

....

[1]

[Total 10 marks]

      Topic C5 — Monitoring and Controlling Chemical Reactions

Reaction Rates

1   A student reacts sulfuric acid with calcium carbonate to form calcium sulfate, water and carbon dioxide gas.   PRACTICAL

a) Outline a method the student could follow to monitor the rate of this reaction.

    ....

    ....

    ....

    ....

    [3]

b) The graph below shows his results. On the graph below, sketch a curve that shows the rate of reaction that would be seen if the experiment was carried out at a higher temperature.

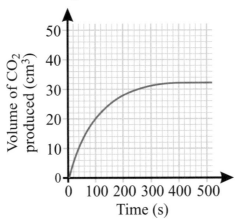

    [1]

c) The scientist carries out the same reaction using different quantities of reactants.
    Reaction **X** used 0.500 g of calcium carbonate and an excess of 0.100 mol/dm^3 sulfuric acid.
    Which of the sets of conditions below could have resulted in reaction **Y**?

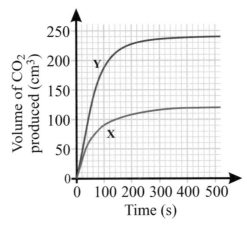

    A   0.250 g of calcium carbonate and an excess of 0.100 mol/dm^3 sulfuric acid.
    B   1.00 g of calcium carbonate and an excess of 0.100 mol/dm^3 sulfuric acid.
    C   0.250 g of calcium carbonate and an excess of 0.200 mol/dm^3 sulfuric acid.
    D   1.00 g of calcium carbonate and an excess of 0.200 mol/dm^3 sulfuric acid.

    Your answer [ ]

    [1]

    [Total 5 marks]

Topic C5 — Monitoring and Controlling Chemical Reactions

2 Shabnam reacted magnesium ribbons with hydrochloric acid. As the reaction proceeded, hydrogen gas was produced.

PRACTICAL

a) Shabnam decides to measure the loss of mass over the course of the reaction.
Draw a labelled diagram to show the apparatus Shabnam could use to follow the rate of this reaction.

[2]

b) Shabnam carried out two different reactions, **M** and **N**, using two different concentrations of hydrochloric acid in order to see how concentration affects the rate of reaction.

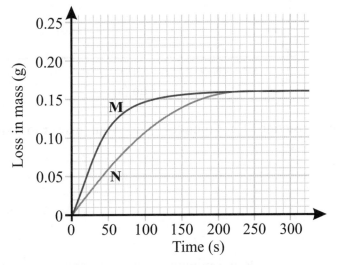

Reaction **N** used a lower concentration of hydrochloric acid.
Using the graph, calculate the rate of reaction N between 0 and 50 seconds.

Rate = ... g/s
[2]

c) Shabnam then reacted magnesium and hydrochloric acid under four temperature conditions, **A**, **B**, **C** and **D**, whilst keeping all other variables the same. Her results are displayed in the following table. Complete the table by calculating the relative rate of each of the reactions.

Temperature	A	B	C	D
Time taken for reaction to stop (s)	243	371	286	435
Relative rate (1/s)	....	....	....	....

[2]

d) Using your results, put the temperatures, A, B, C and D, in order of increasing temperature.

....

[1]

[Total 7 marks]

Topic C5 — Monitoring and Controlling Chemical Reactions

3 A student wanted to calculate the rate of reaction between nitric acid and zinc. He carried out two experiments under the same conditions, but in one he used zinc ribbons and in the other he used zinc powder.

a) The graph below shows the rate of reaction for both experiments, labelled **Q** and **R**.

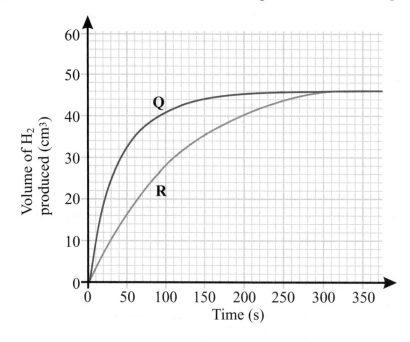

i) Calculate the rate of reaction Q at 3 minutes. Give your answer to 3 significant figures.

Rate = ... cm³/s

[2]

ii) Calculate the rate of reaction **R** at 4 minutes. Give your answer to 3 significant figures.

Rate = ... cm³/s

[2]

b) Determine which reaction, **Q** or **R**, used the powdered zinc. Explain your answer.

....

....

....

[2]

[Total 6 marks]

Exam Practice Tip

Drawing a tangent at a specific point on a curve can be quite tricky. You need to make sure that it has the same gradient of the curve at that specific point. Drawing a tangent too different from the correct gradient could make a big difference to your final answer, so take your time and try moving your ruler around a bit first to find the best position.

Topic C5 — Monitoring and Controlling Chemical Reactions

Collision Theory

1 The Sabatier reaction can be used industrially to make methane from carbon dioxide and hydrogen in the following reaction:

$$CO_{2(g)} + 4H_{2(g)} \rightarrow CH_{4(g)} + 2H_2O_{(g)}$$

a) How could the pressure be altered to **increase** the rate of the reaction?

....

[1]

b) Use the collision theory to explain how this pressure change causes the rate to increase.

....

....

....

[2]

[Total 3 marks]

2 Horatio and Sharon are carrying out an experiment. They each react 50 cm³ of 0.30 mol/dm³ sodium thiosulfate with 5.0 cm³ of 2.0 mol/dm³ hydrochloric acid.

a) Horatio carries out his reaction at room temperature. Sharon heats her reactants to 45 °C and carries out the reaction in a 45 °C water bath. Horatio thinks that his reaction will have taken place much more quickly than Sharon's reaction. Is Horatio correct? Explain your answer.

....

....

....

....

....

[3]

b) i) Sharon repeats her experiment using different concentrations of hydrochloric acid. Which of the following concentrations of hydrochloric acid would result in the **slowest** rate of reaction?

    A   0.350 mol/dm³ hydrochloric acid

    B   1.250 mol/dm³ hydrochloric acid

    C   2.100 mol/dm³ hydrochloric acid

    D   0.550 mol/dm³ hydrochloric acid

Your answer ☐

[1]

ii) Explain your answer.

....

....

[2]

[Total 6 marks]

   Topic C5 — Monitoring and Controlling Chemical Reactions

Catalysts

1 Identify which of the following catalysts is an example of an enzyme.

    A   Iron: a catalyst used in the Haber process.

    B   Manganese(IV) oxide: a catalyst used in the decomposition of hydrogen peroxide.

    C   RuBisCO: a catalyst used in photosynthesis.

    D   Vanadium pentoxide: a catalyst used in the Contact process.

Your answer ☐

[Total 1 mark]

2 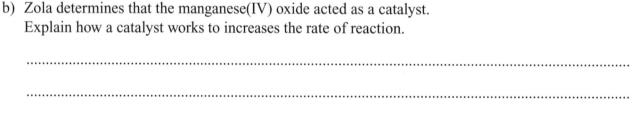 Zola is observing the decomposition of hydrogen peroxide. The reaction is very slow. Meredith tells her to repeat the experiment with manganese(IV) oxide powder, and the rate of reaction increases. Zola hypothesises that the manganese(IV) oxide is a catalyst.

a) Describe how Zola can determine whether or not the manganese(IV) oxide is a catalyst.

....

....

....

....

[2]

b) Zola determines that the manganese(IV) oxide acted as a catalyst.
Explain how a catalyst works to increases the rate of reaction.

....

....

....

[2]

c) The reaction profile for the catalysed and uncatalysed reaction is shown below. Identify what each of the labels, A–D, show.

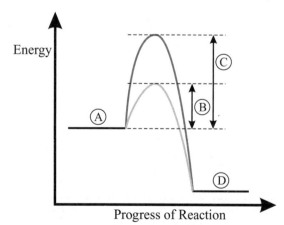

A: ....

B: ....

C: ....

D: ....

[4]

[Total 8 marks]

Topic C5 — Monitoring and Controlling Chemical Reactions

Dynamic Equilibrium

Warm-Up

Choose from the words in the box below to complete the paragraph.

increases	change	the same rate	different rates	decreases	not change

In a reaction, as the concentration of reactants fall, the rate of the forward reaction ....

and as the concentration of the products rises, the rate of the backward reaction ....

When both the forward and backward reaction are going at ...., they are at

equilibrium. At this point, the concentration of the reactants and products will ....

1 Dynamic equilibria can only be achieved in reversible reactions. The position of equilibria can be affected by different factors. *(Grade 4-6)*

a) Give the definition of a reversible reaction.

....

....

[1]

b) During a certain reversible reaction, the equilibrium lies to the left. How should the concentration of the reactants be altered in order to increase the rate of product formation?

....

[1]

[Total 2 marks]

2 Methanol can be manufactured industrially from a gas mixture of mainly carbon monoxide and hydrogen in the following reaction: $CO_{(g)} + 2H_{2(g)} \rightleftharpoons CH_3OH_{(g)}$. This occurs over a Cu-ZnO-Al$_2$O$_3$ catalyst, under conditions of 250 °C and 50–100 atm. The forward reaction is exothermic. *(Grade 6-7)*

a) Under a certain set of conditions, the equilibrium lies to the right. Describe what this means, in terms of the concentration of products and reactants.

....

....

[1]

b) Identify which of the following statements is **false**.

A A decrease in the concentration of CO shifts the position of equilibrium to the left.
B Increasing the pressure to 200 atm shifts the position of equilibrium to the right.
C Increasing the temperature to 470 °C shifts the position of equilibrium to the left.
D The Cu-ZnO-Al$_2$O$_3$ catalyst shifts the position of equilibrium to the right.

Your answer ☐

[1]

[Total 2 marks]

Topic C5 — Monitoring and Controlling Chemical Reactions

3 Nitrogen dioxide forms an equilibrium mixture with dinitrogen tetroxide in the following reaction: $2NO_{2(g)} \rightleftharpoons N_2O_{4(g)}$. The forward reaction is exothermic.

Grade 6-7

a) Which of the following conditions would result in the greatest shift of the equilibrium to the **left**?

A High temperature and high pressure.
B High temperature and low pressure.
C Low temperature and high pressure.
D Low temperature and low pressure.

Your answer ☐

[1]

b) In terms of equilibrium, explain why it is important for the reaction vessel to be completely sealed.

....

....

[1]

[Total 2 marks]

4 An exothermic reaction between potassium thiocyanate and iron(III) nitrate in solution forms an equilibrium mixture: $Fe^{3+}_{(aq)} + SCN^-_{(aq)} \rightleftharpoons [Fe(SCN)]^{2+}_{(aq)}$. Fe^{3+} is orange, SCN^- is colourless and $[Fe(SCN)]^{2+}$ (iron thiocyanate) is red.

Grade 7-9

a) Russell has a solution of iron thiocyanate. He divides the solution equally between four test tubes. The table below shows the treatment given to each of the test tubes. Complete the table by determining the colour of the solution in each condition.

Test Tube	Condition	Colour of solution
A	Control	Red
B	Addition of $[Fe(SCN)]^{2+}$	....
C	Hot water bath	....
D	Ice bath	....

[3]

b) Explain your answer for test tube **C**.

....

....

....

....

[2]

c) Amara says, to increase the yield of the reaction, they should increase the pressure of the reaction. Russell disagrees. Which student do you agree with? Explain your answer.

....

....

[1]

[Total 6 marks]

Topic C5 — Monitoring and Controlling Chemical Reactions

Extracting Metals from their Ores

1   The method used to extract metals from their ores can be determined using the reactivity series. The reactivity series of some elements is shown below.

Potassium	K	Most Reactive
Calcium	Ca	
Aluminium	Al	
Carbon	C	
Zinc	Zn	
Tin	Sn	
Copper	Cu	Least Reactive

a) Give the definition of a metal ore.

....

....
                                                                                        [1]

b) Describe how tin is extracted from its ore in industry.

....

....
                                                                                        [1]

c) State **one** other metal from the reactivity series above that can be extracted in the same way as tin.

....
                                                                                        [1]
                                                                              [Total 3 marks]

2   Iron is extracted from its ore, iron oxide (Fe_2O_3), in a blast furnace using carbon. (Grade 7-9)

a) Write a balanced equation for this reaction.

....
                                                                                        [2]

b) A certain batch of iron ore that contains impurities of zinc oxide and calcium oxide
    is reacted in a blast furnace. After the reaction is complete, any metal produced by
    the reaction was removed. Any unreacted ore was left in the reaction vessel.

    The iron metal product was tested for purity and was found to contain traces of another metal.
    Suggest an identity for the other metal and explain why it's present.

....

....

....

....
                                                                                        [2]
                                                                              [Total 4 marks]

Extracting Metals with Electrolysis

1 A manufacturing company wants to extract a metal for use as a component in a car. After consideration, they decide to use either aluminium or iron.

a) Using the reactivity series below, determine which metal would be more expensive to extract from its ore. Explain your answer.

Aluminium	Al	Most Reactive
Carbon	C	↓
Iron	Fe	Least Reactive

....

....

....

....

....

[4]

b) The company also needs copper wires for the cars' electrical systems. They extract copper from its ore using carbon in a blast furnace.

State why the copper needs to undergo purification before it can be used for electrical wires and name the process used to purify it.

....

....

[2]

[Total 6 marks]

2 The increasing demand and the limited supply of metal-rich ores means that scientists are now developing new ways to extract metal from low-grade ores.

a) Describe how phytoextraction is used to extract some metals from their ores.

....

....

....

....

....

[4]

b) Give **one** advantage and **one** disadvantage of using phytoextraction to extract metals from their ores.

....

....

[2]

[Total 6 marks]

Alloys

1   Alloys have properties that can make them more useful than pure metals.   (Grade 4-6)

   a) Give the definition of an alloy.

   ....

   ....
                                                                                                              [1]

   b) Steel is an alloy made from iron and carbon, frequently used in construction.
       Give **one** advantage of using steel over iron in construction.

   ....
                                                                                                              [1]

   c) Bronze is an alloy made from copper and tin.
       Which of the following statements about the properties of bronze is **true**?

       A   Bronze is much softer than tin.
       B   Bronze is more resistant to corrosion than copper or tin.
       C   The low density of bronze makes it suitable for building aircraft.
       D   Tin and copper are stronger than bronze.

       Your answer ☐

                                                                                                              [1]
                                                                                                [Total 3 marks]

2   The table below shows the melting points of several materials.   (Grade 7-9)

Material	Melting point (°C)
Duralumin	650
Solder ($Sn_{60}Pb_{40}$)	183 – 188
Tin	232
Zinc	420

Suggest which material from the table would be the **most** suitable for
joining metal components in a circuit board. Explain your answer.

   ....

   ....

   ....

   ....
                                                                                                [Total 2 marks]

Corrosion

1 Martha and Joe both own bikes with iron bike chains. Martha leaves her bike outside and, after a week, discovers that the chain has started to rust.

Grade 6-7

a) Write the word equation for the reaction that takes place when iron rusts.

....

[2]

b) Joe keeps his bike inside. Is his bike more or less likely to rust than Martha's? Explain your answer.

....

....

[2]

c) i) Martha buys a new iron bike chain. From the choice below, chose the **best** method that she could use to prevent her new chain from rusting?

    A   Painting
    B   Oiling
    C   Tin plating
    D   Galvanisation

    Your answer ☐   *[1]*

ii) Explain your answer.

....

....

[2]

[Total 7 marks]

2 There are several methods that can be used to prevent the corrosion of metals and alloys.

Grade 7-9

a) A ship manufacturer wants to prevent the corrosion of a ship's steel hull by bolting blocks of metal to the hull. Should the manufacturer use tin or magnesium blocks to stop the hull corroding? Explain your answer.

....

....

....

....

[3]

b) A roofing company coats an iron roof with a layer of zinc to protect it from rusting.
After a while, the zinc layer becomes scratched.
Would you expect the iron roofing to begin to rust? Explain your answer.

....

....

[1]

[Total 4 marks]

The Haber Process

1 The Haber process is an important industrial process. **Grade 4-6**

a) Give the balanced symbol equation for the reaction that occurs in the Haber process.

....
[3]

b) Give **one** use of the product(s) made during the Haber process.

....
[1]

[Total 4 marks]

2 The Haber process is carried out at a pressure of 200 atm and a temperature of 450 °C. **Grade 7-9**

a) i) A company increases the temperature in the reaction vessel for the Haber process to 580 °C. Which of the following is the result of this change in temperature?

    A   Higher rate of reaction.
    B   Lower rate of reaction.
    C   No change in the rate of reaction.
    D   Rate of reaction is halved.

Your answer ☐
[1]

ii) The company thinks the increase in temperature will increase the yield of product from the Haber process. Do you agree or disagree with the company? Explain your answer.

....

....

....
[2]

b) In a bid to make the process cheaper, the company decides to reduce the pressure at which they carry out the Haber process.

Give **two** disadvantages of using a low pressure to carry out the Haber process.

....

....
[2]

c) The Haber process uses an iron catalyst. How does the iron catalyst affect:

i) the rate? ....
[1]

ii) the yield? ....
[1]

[Total 7 marks]

Topic C6 — Global Challenges

88

Fertilisers

Use the words below to complete the sentences to describe how ammonium nitrate is made. You won't need to use all of the words.

| Nitrogen | Nitric acid | Haber Process | Hydrocarbons | Ammonium nitrate | Sulfuric acid |

Hydrogen can be obtained from .... and .... is extracted from the air. These two substances are reacted together in the .... to produce ammonia. Ammonia and .... are then reacted together to make the fertiliser, ...

1   Fertilisers are salts produced by reacting an acid with a base.   Grade 4-6

   a) Give the names of the acid and the base that are used to make ammonium phosphate in industry.

   ....
   [1]

   b) Give the names of the acid and the base that can be used to make potassium nitrate.

   ....
   [1]

   [Total 2 marks]

PRACTICAL

2   A student is creating a sample of ammonium sulfate crystals using a titrimetric method. She adds ammonia to a sulfuric acid and indicator solution until there is a colour change. The student then crystallises the solution and is left with impure ammonium sulfate crystals.   Grade 6-7

   a) Suggest a piece of equipment that she could use to add the ammonia solution to the acid.

   ....
   [1]

   b) What should the student have done to produce pure ammonium sulfate crystals?

   ....
   ....
   ....
   [2]

   c) Give **one** reason why factories do **not** use this laboratory method to produce ammonium sulfate.

   ....
   ....
   [1]

   [Total 4 marks]

Topic C6 — Global Challenges

The Contact Process

1   The Contact process is an industrial process involving three separate stages.

$$\textbf{Step 1}:\ S + O_2 \rightarrow SO_2$$
$$\textbf{Step 2}:\ 2SO_2 + O_2 \rightleftharpoons 2SO_3$$
$$\textbf{Step 3}:\ SO_3 + H_2O \rightarrow H_2SO_4$$

Why is it important that the conditions are controlled in **Step 2** of the Contact process?

....

....

[Total 2 marks]

2   A fertiliser manufacturer uses the Contact process to produce sulfuric acid. The second step of the Contact process involves the oxidation of sulfur dioxide, which is an exothermic process.

$$2SO_2 + O_2 \rightleftharpoons 2SO_3$$

a) The company must maintain suitable conditions for this reaction to be economical.
Identify the statement below that is **false**.

   A   Higher pressures will increase the yield of SO_3.
   B   Lower pressures are cheaper to maintain.
   C   High pressures will increase the rate of reaction.
   D   Using lower pressures increases the reaction rate.

Your answer ☐

[1]

b) A fault with the system causes the temperature in the reaction vessel to decrease from 450 °C to 210 °C. Discuss how and why this change in temperature would affect:

i) the yield of the reaction.

     ....

     ....

     ....

[2]

ii) the rate of the reaction.

     ....

     ....

     ....

[3]

[Total 6 marks]

Exam Practice Tip

When a reaction is reversible, you want to maximise the yield of the desired product whilst keeping the rate of reaction as high as possible. To make things harder, this all needs to be done whilst keeping the costs down. So, if you're asked about the best conditions for a reversible reaction, think about all three of these factors before jumping to any conclusions.

Topic C6 — Global Challenges

Industrial Processes

1 An industrial company is researching the implications of using crude oil as a starting material. *(Grade 4-6)*

a) Give **one** disadvantage of using crude oil as a source of raw materials.

....

[1]

b) A company discovers it can synthesise a crude oil substitute using a reaction that occurs at high temperatures and pressures. Suggest why using the crude oil substitute as a starting material may not be economically viable.

....

....

[1]

[Total 2 marks]

2 The graph below shows the effect of pH and temperature on the rate of a reaction. *(Grade 7-9)*

a) From the conditions shown on the graph, what is the optimum pH and temperature for the reaction to maximise the rate?

pH = ...   Temperature = ...

[2]

b) The yield of this reaction is at its highest when the temperature is 10 °C. Explain whether it is sensible to carry the reaction out at this temperature or not.

....

....

[1]

c) The company decide to increase the pressure that they carry this reaction out at. Give **one** advantage and **one** disadvantage of increasing the pressure.

....

....

....

[2]

[Total 5 marks]

Life-Cycle Assessments

A company is developing a new product. Identify the factors that they should consider when producing a life-cycle assessment. Tick **two** boxes.

Colour of the product ☐   Demand for the product ☐

Recyclability of the product ☐   Attractiveness of the product ☐

Source of raw materials ☐   Profitability of the product ☐

1   A furniture company is designing a new range of chairs for children.
They need to decide whether the chair will be made out of polypropene or timber.

Grade 6-7

Material	Source	Relative Energy Cost to Make/Extract	Recyclability
Timber	Trees	1	Recyclable
Polypropene	Crude oil	15	Recyclable

a)   The company carries out a life-cycle assessment of both possible products.
Describe the purpose of a life-cycle assessment.

....

....

[1]

b)   Using the table above, explain which material would be the **best** choice
to make the table from, in terms of sustainability. Explain your answer.

....

....

....

....

....

[3]

c)   Suggest **two** further factors, that aren't discussed in the table, that the company should consider in
their life-cycle assessment, when deciding whether to make the chairs from timber or polypropene.

....

....

[2]

[Total 6 marks]

2 A toy company is carrying out a life-cycle assessment of four prototype toys. The table below displays some of the data from their assessments.

 Grade 7-9

Toy	CO_2 emissions (kg)	Solvent use (dm^3)	Consumption of non-renewable energy (MJ)
A	16.2	3981	267.84
B	14.8	2672	212.26
C	14.9	3876	159.82
D	12.4	2112	174.56

a) Using the data in the table, explain which toy, A, B, C or D, the company should produce.

....

....

....

....

....

....

[4]

b) Toy A contains components made from iron. Iron is found naturally as iron oxide in the ground. Give **two** disadvantages associated with extracting iron.

....

....

[2]

c) All of the toys contain components that cannot be recycled, so the company suggests that at the end of their life spans, the toys should be disposed of in landfill. Explain why the use of landfill as a form of disposal is **unsustainable**.

....

[1]

d) Several of the toys are sold in plastic packaging. Which of the options below describes the best way to dispose of this packaging, in terms of sustainability?

A Dispose of the waste in nearby rivers.
B Bury the waste in landfill.
C Recycle the waste into different products.
D Incinerate the waste.

Your answer ☐

[1]

[Total 8 marks]

Exam Practice Tip

You may be given data and asked to figure out which product has the biggest or smallest environmental impact. It's likely that there won't be an obvious answer at first glance — some products may have really low CO_2 emissions but may pollute lots of water. You'll have to look at all the factors and decide which product is the best or worst overall.

Topic C6 — Global Challenges

Recycling Materials

1   Rachel is sorting some rubbish that has accumulated around her house.

a) Rachel has three pieces of rubbish made from three different materials, A, B and C.
Some data about the materials is in the table below.

Material	Availability of resource	Energy to recycle	Energy to extract
A	Abundant	High	Low
B	Limited	Low	High
C	Limited	Medium	High

Which material from the table above is the **best** to recycle? Explain your answer.

....

....

....

....
                                                                                                    [2]

b) Rachel is able to recycle plastic bottles at her local recycling centre.
Given that many parts of the manufacturing process involve using fractions of crude oil,
explain why it is important to recycle plastics.

....

....
                                                                                                    [1]

c)   i) Rachel has a drinks carton that is made from a paper box with a plastic coating and an
aluminium cap. Suggest why it might **not** be economical to recycle the drinks carton.

....

....
                                                                                                    [1]

ii) Rachel decides to recycle the drinks carton since it contains non-renewable materials.
Which materials in the drinks carton come from **non-renewable** sources?

A   Paper, plastic and aluminium.
B   Paper and plastic.
C   Aluminium only.
D   Plastic and aluminium.

Your answer [ ]
                                                                                                    [1]

iii) Give **one** use for the recycled paper from the drinks carton.

....
                                                                                                    [1]

                                                                                    [Total 6 marks]

                      Topic C6 — Global Challenges

Types of Materials and their Uses

1 Materials can be categorised into several different types. (Grade 4-6)

a) Match each of the materials with the group of materials it belongs to.

Glass	Metal
Polystyrene	Polymer
Aluminium	Composite
Fibreglass	Ceramic

[4]

b) Describe what a composite material is and explain what determines their properties.

....

....

[2]

[Total 6 marks]

2 The uses of materials are determined by their properties. (Grade 6-7)

a) The table below shows the properties of some materials.

Material	Flexibility	Electrical Conductivity	Cost
Plasticised PVC	Very good	Low	Low
HDPE	Poor	Low	Low
Aluminium	Good	High	Medium

Which material would be the **most** suitable for covering electrical wires to insulate them? Explain your answer.

....

....

....

[3]

b) High density polyethene and low-density polyethene have different physical properties due to the arrangement of the polymer chains in the bulk material. Predict whether high-density polyethene or low-density polyethene is **better** for making a shampoo bottle. Explain your answer.

....

....

....

[2]

[Total 5 marks]

3   The table below shows the properties of several different materials.

Material	Density (g/cm³)	Strength (MPa)	Resistance to Corrosion	Cost
PVC	1.3	52	Good	Low
Carbon fibre	1.5	4100	Good	High
Copper	8.9	220	Poor	Medium
Steel	7.8	780	Poor (but can be easily protected)	Low
Lead	11.3	12	Good	Low

a) A sports company is deciding on the best material for making a professional hockey stick.
    Which material from the table would be the **most** suitable?
    Use the data from the table to explain your answer.

    ....

    ....

    ....

    ....

    ....

                                                                                                    [4]

b) Determine which material from the table is the **most** suitable for building bridges.
    Explain your answer using information from the table.

    ....

    ....

    ....

    ....

    ....

                                                                                                    [4]

c) Determine which material from the table would be the **most** suitable material to make drain pipes.
    Explain your answer using information from the table.

    ....

    ....

    ....

    ....

                                                                                                    [4]
                                                                                        [Total 12 marks]

Exam Practice Tip

You may need to decide, out of a choice of materials, which one is the most suitable for making something. Although physical properties are important, don't forget to look at cost. For example, carbon fibre is very strong but also very expensive — if you need to use a lot of it, like for building bridges, it'll cost a lot and this can sometimes be a problem.

                      Topic C6 — Global Challenges

Alkanes and Alkenes

1 Alkanes are a homologous series of hydrocarbons.

a) i) Name the alkane that contains two carbon atoms.

....
[1]

ii) State the number of hydrogen atoms that this alkane contains.

....
[1]

b) Draw the displayed formula of butane.

[1]
[Total 3 marks]

2 A student is investigating the chemical structure of alkenes.

a) Give the general formula for alkenes.

....
[1]

b) Identify the displayed formula below that shows ethene.

A   H—C—C—H (H H top, H H bottom)

B   C=C—C (ethene-like with extra C)

C   C=C (ethene)

D   H—C—C—C—H (H H H top and bottom)

Your answer ☐

[1]

c) Methane is an alkane with one carbon atom. The student notices that there is not an alkene with only one carbon atom. Explain why an alkene with one carbon atom does **not** exist.

....

....
[1]
[Total 3 marks]

3 The combustion of an alkane occurs when the alkane is burned in oxygen. Combustion can be either complete or incomplete.

a) Describe the cause of the incomplete combustion of an alkane.

....

[1]

b) Give the balanced symbol equation for the incomplete combustion of propane, forming carbon monoxide and water only.

....

[2]

[Total 3 marks]

4 A student was investigating the reactivity of some hydrocarbons in the lab.

a) The student added a sample of a hydrocarbon, **A**, to bromine water and allowed it to react. The chemical formula of the product formed was $C_3H_6Br_2$. Draw the displayed formula of the original hydrocarbon, **A**.

[1]

b) What would the student see happen when the hydrocarbon, **A**, was added to the bromine water, and was then allowed to react?

....

[1]

c) In a separate experiment, bromine water was added to a sample of butene and a reaction occurred. Which of the following structures **could** have been formed by the reaction?

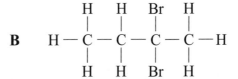

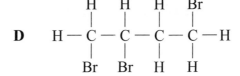

Your answer ☐

[1]

d) Butene reacts with hydrogen as part of a hydrogenation reaction. State the name of the product formed by this reaction.

....

[1]

[Total 4 marks]

Topic C6 — Global Challenges

Alcohols

Warm-Up

Identify which of the following functional groups represents alcohols. Tick **one** box.

C=C ☐   -COO⁻ ☐

-NO₂ ☐   -OH ☐

-COOH ☐   -NH₃ ☐

1 Alcohols are a series of organic compounds with a wide range of industrial applications. **(Grade 4-6)**

a) An alcohol containing 3 carbons is commonly used as a solvent.
What is the name given to this alcohol?

....
[1]

b) Ethanol is present in alcoholic drinks. Give the chemical formula for ethanol.

....
[1]

c) Methanol can be used as an additive to fuels to improve combustion.
Draw the displayed formula for methanol.

[1]
[Total 3 marks]

2 Under certain conditions, alcohols can be oxidised to form carboxylic acids. **(Grade 4-6)**

a) What is the functional group of a carboxylic acid?

....
[1]

b) Give the chemical formula for propanoic acid.

....
[1]

c) Name the carboxylic acid with the chemical formula CH_3COOH.

....
[1]
[Total 3 marks]

3 Three of the following structures belong to the same homologous series. Identify the structure that belongs to a **different** homologous series.

A
$$H-\underset{\underset{H}{|}}{\overset{\overset{H}{|}}{C}}-\underset{\underset{H}{|}}{\overset{\overset{H}{|}}{C}}-C\overset{\displaystyle{/\!\!/O}}{\underset{\displaystyle{\diagdown O-H}}{}}$$

B
$$H-\underset{\underset{H}{|}}{\overset{\overset{H}{|}}{C}}-\underset{\underset{H}{|}}{\overset{\overset{H}{|}}{C}}-O-H$$

C
$$H-\underset{\underset{\displaystyle{\underset{|}{O}}}{|}}{\overset{\overset{H}{|}}{C}}-H$$
$$\underset{H}{}$$

D
$$H-\underset{\underset{H}{|}}{\overset{\overset{H}{|}}{C}}-\underset{\underset{H}{|}}{\overset{\overset{O}{|}}{C}}-\underset{\underset{H}{|}}{\overset{\overset{H}{|}}{C}}-H$$

Your answer ☐

[Total 1 mark]

4 Two organic molecules, **Y** and **Z**, are added to separate test tubes and reacted with an oxidising agent. The reaction mixture in one test tube changes from purple to colourless, the reaction mixture in the other test tube remains purple.

a) What was the oxidising agent used in the reaction?

....
[1]

b) The two possible organic molecules are shown below. Identify which molecule, **Y** or **Z**, reacted to form the colourless solution. Explain your answer.

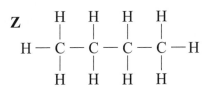

....

....

....

....

....
[4]

c) Draw the displayed formula of the organic product that was formed in the reaction where the solution lost its colour.

[1]

[Total 6 marks]

Topic C6 — Global Challenges

Addition Polymerisation

1 The following question is about addition polymers.

a) Which of these homologous series can form addition polymers?

    A   alkenes and alkanes

    B   alkenes only

    C   carboxylic acids only

    D   alcohols and carboxylic acids

Your answer ☐

[1]

b) The formula of vinyl acetate is shown to the right.
Vinyl acetate polymerises to form polyvinyl acetate.
Draw the formula of the repeating unit of polyvinyl acetate.

[1]

c) The formula of one repeating unit of polypropene is shown
to the right. Draw the formula of its monomer.

[1]

d) The addition polymer polyvinyl chloride, PVC, can be represented by the notation $(C_2H_3Cl)_n$.
Draw the displayed formula for the monomer that polymerises to form PVC.

[1]

[Total 4 marks]

2 Tamwar is making polystyrene in the laboratory. He heats a sample of phenylethene and an initiator in a beaker using a Bunsen burner. He heats the mixture for a total of three minutes.

a) Identify and explain **two** improvements that Tamwar should make to the method he uses.

....

....

....

....

[2]

b) Why does Tamwar need to use an initiator?

....

....

[1]

[Total 3 marks]

3 A class are carrying out an investigation to look at monomers and addition polymers.

a) The students evaluate the monomer methyl methacrylate. This monomer is shown to the right. Selena believes that it can form an addition polymer but Jenna disagrees. State which student you agree with and why.

....

....

[1]

b) The students study polytetrafluoroethene, PTFE, a polymer commonly used in cookware. The repeating unit of this polymer is shown to the right. Which of the monomers below forms the polymer, polytetrafluoroethene?

A
```
     F   F
     |   |
 H — C — C — H
     |   |
     F   F
```

B
```
  F         F
   \       /
    C  =  C
   /       \
  F         F
```

C
```
  F         F
   \       /
    C  =  C
   /       \
  H         H
```

D
```
     F   F
     |   |
 H — C — C — H
     |   |
     H   H
```

Your answer [ ]

[1]

[Total 2 marks]

Exam Practice Tip

The monomers of addition polymers must have a C=C bond, but in polymer form this double bond becomes a single bond. Carbon always has four bonds, so if you're drawing the repeating unit of a polymer, count how many bonds your carbon atoms have. This way, you can check the bonds to make sure they're all present and correct.

Topic C6 — Global Challenges

Condensation Polymerisation

1 Some condensation polymers occur naturally and are essential to our growth and survival.

a) DNA is formed from two strands of nucleotide monomers. Name the **four** nucleotide bases.

....

[2]

b) Proteins are a form of polyamide. Name the type of monomer which forms proteins.

....

[1]

[Total 3 marks]

2 Some polymers are made by condensation polymerisation.

a) The structure of propylamine is shown below.
Is this molecule able to form condensation polymers or not? Explain your answer.

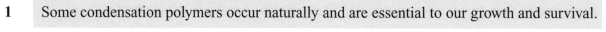

....

....

....

....

[2]

b) Identify the pair of reactants that would react to form a polyester.

Your answer [ ]

[1]

[Total 3 marks]

3 Nylon-6,6 is a condensation polymer that can be made both in the lab and in industry using two different reactions.

a) In industry, nylon-6,6 is made using hexanedioic acid and 1,6 diaminohexane. These reactants are shown below.

What type of condensation polymer is nylon-6,6?

....

[1]

b) Draw a block diagram to represent the repeating unit of this polymer.

[2]

c) A student is making nylon-6,6 in the lab. He has one beaker containing a solution of 1,6-diaminohexane in water and a separate beaker containing a solution of 1,6-hexanediol dichloride in an organic solvent. The two monomers are shown below.

Describe a method that the student should follow to make and collect nylon-6,6 from these two solutions.

....

....

....

....

[4]

d) Look at the reactants used in the industrial and laboratory reactions to prepare nylon-6,6. How would you expect the by-products of both of these reactions differ?

....

....

[2]

[Total 9 marks]

Topic C6 — Global Challenges

Crude Oil

Warm-Up

Use a line to match each of the following fractions of crude oil with one of their main uses.

Naphtha	Fuel for aircraft
Diesel	Raw material in industrial processes
Kerosene	Fuel for lorries

1 Crude oil is our main source of hydrocarbons. *Grade 4-6*

a) Describe how crude oil is formed.

....

....

....

[2]

b) Crude oil is a mixture of a variety of hydrocarbons. Give the general formula
   of the homologous series which makes up a majority of these hydrocarbons.

....

[1]

[Total 3 marks]

2 Today's society is crucially dependent on crude oil as a source of energy, however,
   a variety of alternative energy sources are being developed by scientists. *Grade 6-7*

a) Give **two** reasons why the Earth's usage of fossil fuels is increasing.

....

....

[2]

b) Name **two** alternative sources of energy.

....

[2]

c) Why it is important that scientists develop alternative energy sources?

....

....

[1]

[Total 5 marks]

3 Crude oil can be separated using the process of fractional distillation. The length of the hydrocarbon chains is fundamental to this process.

Grade 7-9

a) Outline the process of fractional distillation.

....

....

....

....

....

....

[4]

b) i) Name the fraction of crude oil which contains the **shortest** hydrocarbon chains.

....

[1]

ii) Name **one** other fraction that is produced by the fractional distillation of crude oil.

....

[1]

c) The table below shows the boiling points of some molecules that are present in fractions produced when crude oil is fractionated.

Hydrocarbon	Chemical formula	Boiling point (°C)
Heptane	C_7H_{16}	98
Triacontane	$C_{30}H_{62}$	343

i) Which hydrocarbon would you expect to be collected **further down** the column?

....

[1]

ii) Explain your answer, with reference to the intermolecular bonding present between the hydrocarbons.

....

....

....

....

....

....

[5]

[Total 12 marks]

Topic C6 — Global Challenges

Cracking

1 Cracking involves splitting long-chain hydrocarbons into smaller molecules. *(Grade 4-6)*

a) Explain why cracking is important.

....

....

[2]

b) Name the catalyst used for cracking in industry.

....

[1]

c) Two products were formed by cracking a hydrocarbon. The chemical formulas for the two products were $C_{15}H_{32}$ and C_5H_{10}. Give the chemical formula for the original hydrocarbon.

....

[1]

[Total 4 marks]

2 Hydrocarbon fractions, produced by the fractional distillation of crude oil, are important chemicals used in many industrial processes. The graph below shows the approximate percentage of each fraction produced by an oil refinery, and the demand for each fraction. *(Grade 6-7)*

Fraction obtained from crude oil

a) The demand for diesel is greater than the supply.
Name **two** other fractions whose demand is greater than their supply.

....

[2]

b) Suggest what could be done to ensure that the supply of diesel matches the demand.

....

....

[1]

[Total 3 marks]

Fuel Cells

1 Fuel cells are an alternative way of producing energy, instead of burning crude oil. **Grade 6-7**

a) Give the definition of a fuel cell.

....

....

[2]

b) Which of the following statements about fuel cells is **correct**?

   A   Fuel cells produce a potential difference indefinitely.
   B   Fuel cells produce a potential difference until the reactants are completely used up.
   C   Fuel cells start to produce a potential difference once all the reactants are used up.
   D   Fuel cells produce a potential difference until the reactants are partly used up.

   Your answer ☐

[1]

[Total 3 marks]

2 The hydrogen-oxygen fuel cell contains an electrolyte, an anode and a cathode. **Grade 7-9**

a) Name the electrolyte that is often used in hydrogen-oxygen fuel cells.

....

[1]

b) Explain why the reaction in a hydrogen-oxygen fuel cell can be classified as a redox reaction.

....

....

....

....

....

[4]

c) i) George is investigating the advantages and disadvantages of hydrogen-oxygen fuel cells.
   Give **one** disadvantage associated with using hydrogen-oxygen fuel cells as an energy source.

....

[1]

   ii) George states that we shouldn't use hydrogen-oxygen fuel cells as
   they produce harmful waste chemicals. Comment on George's answer,
   with reference to any chemical produced by hydrogen-oxygen fuel cells.

....

....

[2]

[Total 8 marks]

Topic C6 — Global Challenges

The Atmosphere

1 Which of the following gases was **not** present in the early atmosphere? (Grade 4-6)

    A   water vapour

    B   ammonia

    C   ozone

    D   methane

Your answer ☐

[Total 1 mark]

2 Scientists have looked at the composition of other planets to provide evidence for what the early atmosphere on Earth was like. (Grade 7-9)
The table below shows the compositions of the atmospheres on Mars and Earth.

	Percentage composition (%)					
	H_2O	Ne	CO_2	N_2	O_2	Ar
Mars	0.030	trace	95	2.7	0.13	1.6
Earth	0–4.0	0.0018	0.036	78	21	0.93

a) i) Scientists believe Earth's early atmosphere was similar to the atmosphere on Mars. Using the table, suggest which gas made up the majority of Earth's early atmosphere.

    ....

[1]

  ii) Explain **two** ways in which this gas was removed from Earth's atmosphere as it evolved.

    ....

    ....

[2]

b) Explain how oxygen built up in Earth's atmosphere and suggest why there is hardly any oxygen present in the atmosphere on Mars.

    ....

    ....

    ....

[2]

c) i) Which gas is present in the **highest** concentration in the Earth's atmosphere today?

    ....

[1]

  ii) Explain how and why this gas built up in the Earth's atmosphere.

    ....

    ....

    ....

[3]

[Total 9 marks]

The Greenhouse Effect and Global Warming

Warm-Up

Identify the statements below that describe things that a family can do to reduce their carbon dioxide emissions. Tick **two** boxes.

Leaving lights on all day ☐   Using a tumble drier ☐

Walking to school ☐   Installing solar panels at home ☐

Turning the heating up ☐   Using air conditioning ☐

1 Which statement about alternative fuels is **false**? (Grade 4-6)

    A Ethanol can be mixed with petrol to produce a better fuel.
    B Ethanol is made by the fermentation of plants.
    C Biodiesel and ethanol are carbon neutral.
    D Biodiesel is cheap to produce.

Your answer ☐

[Total 1 mark]

2 Many scientists believe that the increased levels of greenhouse gases, such as carbon dioxide, has resulted in global warming. (Grade 6-7)

a) Give the definition of a greenhouse gas.

....

....
[1]

b) Apart from carbon dioxide, list **two** further greenhouse gases.

....
[2]

c) Elvis states that any greenhouse effect is dangerous as it could cause global warming. Is Elvis correct? Explain your answer.

....

....

....
[1]

d) Global warming is a type of climate change. Give **two** environmental consequences associated with global warming.

....

....
[2]

[Total 6 marks]

Topic C6 — Global Challenges

3 Some scientists believe that the increased burning of fossil fuels has contributed to global warming and this has caused glaciers to melt, thus resulting in rising sea levels. Other scientists believe that the rises in global temperature are just natural fluctuations.

The graph below shows CO_2 emissions by fossil fuels in the UK and the changes in sea levels between 1993 and 2013.

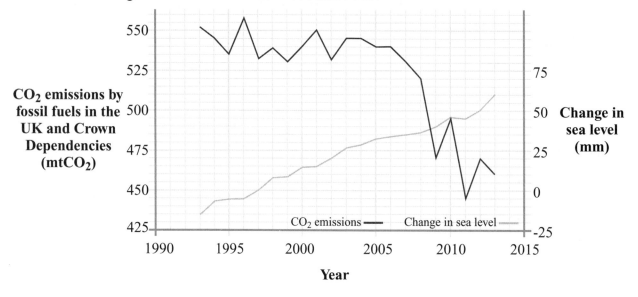

a)* Look at the graph. Explain whether the evidence shown by this graph supports a link between anthropogenic activity and climate change, and discuss any uncertainty associated with the conclusion you can draw from this data.

....

....

....

....

....

....

....

....

[6]

b) Many governments are trying to decrease their countries global CO_2 emissions. Give **two** ways that the government in the UK is trying to reduce carbon dioxide emissions.

....

....

[2]

[Total 8 marks]

Exam Practice Tip

You could be given data that shows a link between human activity and global warming. But, just because there might be a correlation, it doesn't necessarily mean that one causes the other. You need to evaluate what the data actually shows without making assumptions, for example, if you're given data for one country, you can't assume it's had a global effect.

Topic C6 — Global Challenges

Pollutants

1 Carbon monoxide is a gas that is toxic to humans. (Grade 4-6)

a) Explain why carbon monoxide is toxic.

....

....

....

[2]

b) How is carbon monoxide produced?

A By incomplete combustion in car engines.
B By complete combustion in car engines.
C By nitrogen and oxygen reacting together due to the heat of combustion reactions.
D By reactions between carbon and oxygen in car engines.

Your answer ☐

[1]

[Total 3 marks]

2 The table below shows the concentration of pollutants in two cities, **A** and **B**. (Grade 6-7)

City	Concentration of Pollutants (µg/m³)			
	Nitrogen dioxide	**Ozone**	**Particulate carbon**	**Sulfur dioxide**
A	13.2	53.6	65.1	8.9
B	106.4	84.5	13.2	68.2

a) In one city, the buildings have become covered with a black powder.
Suggest which city this has happened in and why it has occurred.

....

....

[2]

b) Give **two** risks to human health associated with high levels of ground level ozone.

....

....

[2]

c) Limestone buildings in one of the cities have become damaged as a result
of chemical weathering. Which of the cities, **A** or **B**, is this likely to have
occurred in? Explain your answer using evidence from the table.

....

....

....

[2]

[Total 6 marks]

Topic C6 — Global Challenges

Water Treatment

1   Fresh water in the UK comes from different sources and is used for drinking, domestic use and industrial processes. Identify which of the following statements is **incorrect**.
Grade 4-6

   A   Water can be used as a cheap raw material in industry.
   B   Water in the UK can be obtained from treated waste water.
   C   Water can be used as a coolant for industrial processes.
   D   Water can be sourced from groundwater, which comes from lakes and rivers.

   Your answer ☐

[Total 1 mark]

2   A purification plant uses multiple steps to purify water. Grade 6-7

   a) The purification plant uses aluminium sulfate during the sedimentation step.
       How does the aluminium sulfate contribute to the purification process?

       ....

       ....
       [1]

   b) The purification process ends with chlorination. Explain what happens during this process.

       ....

       ....
       [1]
       [Total 2 marks]

3   The way that countries source their water is dependent on a variety of factors.
     The table below shows the average annual rainfall in the UK and Kuwait. Grade 6-7

Country	Average annual rainfall (mm)
UK	1129
Kuwait	120

   a) One of these countries gets large quantities of its water by distilling sea water.
       Suggest which country and explain your answer.

       ....

       ....

       ....
       [2]

   b) Give **one** disadvantage of using this process to purify large quantities of drinking water.

       ....
       [1]
       [Total 3 marks]

Mixed Questions

1 Fractional distillation separates crude oil into fractions.
Which of the following fractions is extracted **above** petrol in the fractionating column?

(Grade 4-6)

   A   Kerosene
   B   LPG
   C   Diesel
   D   Naphtha

Your answer ☐

[Total 1 mark]

2 Look at the diagram below. It shows the displayed formula of an organic compound.

(Grade 4-6)

a) Which homologous series does this compound belong to?

....
[1]

b) What is the name of this compound?

....
[1]

c) Find the relative formula mass of this compound.

relative formula mass = ...
[2]

d) What is the empirical formula of this compound?

....
[1]

[Total 5 marks]

3 Stuart mixes lithium hydroxide solution, LiOH, with hydrobromic acid, HBr. The reaction produces a salt and water.

a) Give the name and formula of the salt this reaction would produce.

Name: ....

Formula: ....

[2]

b) Neither of the reactants were in excess.
What would be the pH of the resulting solution?

....

[1]

c) Stuart wants to confirm the identities of his original reactants.

i) Outline a test he could use to confirm the presence of lithium ions in lithium hydroxide. Include any observations you would expect him to make.

....

....

....

[2]

ii) Outline a test he could use to confirm the presence of bromide ions in hydrobromic acid. Include any observations you would expect him to make.

....

....

....

[2]

[Total 7 marks]

4 When calcium metal is added to a solution of copper(II) nitrate, $Cu(NO_3)_2$, a displacement reaction takes place.

a) Write a balanced symbol equation for this reaction.

....

[2]

b) This reaction is a redox reaction.
Identify the oxidising agent and the reducing agent in this reaction.

Oxidising agent: ....

Reducing agent: ....

[1]

[Total 3 marks]

Mixed Questions

5   Sulfur dioxide, SO_2, is formed by the combustion of sulfur.   (Grade 4-6)

a) i)   Name **one** source of sulfur dioxide air pollution.

....

....

[1]

ii) Give **one** way in which sulfur dioxide pollution can create a hazard to the environment.

....

....

[1]

b)   Sulfur dioxide reacts with oxygen gas to form sulfur trioxide, SO_3.
Write a balanced symbol equation for this reaction.

....

[2]

[Total 4 marks]

6   A solution of a metal salt is electrolysed.
During the electrolysis, a gas is produced at each electrode.   (Grade 6-7)

a)   The gases produced at the electrodes are collected and tested.

i)   The gas produced at the anode is found to relight a glowing splint.
What is the gas produced at the **anode**?

....

[1]

ii) The gas produced at the cathode is found to burn with a squeaky pop.
What is the gas produced at the **cathode**?

....

[1]

b)   The salt in the solution is composed of a metal ion and a non-metal ion.

i)   What do the identities of the gases produced during the electrolysis
tell you about the reactivity of the **metal** that forms the ions in the salt?

....

....

[1]

ii) What do the identities of the gases produced during the electrolysis
tell you about the identity of the **non-metal ion** in the salt?

....

....

[1]

[Total 4 marks]

Mixed Questions

7   Look at the table. It lists some properties of four materials.

Material	Density (g/cm^3)	Brittleness	Corrosion resistance	Cost
Titanium	4.5	Low	High	Very high
Duralumin	2.8	Low	Low	Moderate
Melamine resin	1.5	Moderate	High	Low
Glass	2.5	Very high	High	Low

a) Titanium and duralumin both have a metallic structure.
   Suggest **one** similarity you would expect in the physical properties of titanium and duralumin, other than the properties mentioned in the table.
   Explain your answer in terms of their structure and bonding.

   ....

   ....

   ....

   ....

                                                                                                                                            [2]

b) Titanium is a transition metal.
   Give **two** typical properties of transition metals which are **not** common to all metals.

   1. ....

   2. ....

                                                                                                                                            [2]

c) A camping supplies company wants to make low-cost cups for people to use on camping holidays.
   Suggest which of the materials listed in the table would be **most** suitable for this purpose.
   Explain your answer.

   ....

   ....

   ....

   ....

   ....

   ....

   ....

   ....

   ....

                                                                                                                                            [4]

                                                                                                                        [Total 8 marks]

8 Rubidium is an element from Group 1 of the periodic table.
Fluorine is an element from Group 7.
Rubidium metal, Rb, and fluorine gas, F_2, react violently to produce a single product.

Grade 6-7

a) Write a balanced symbol equation for the reaction of rubidium metal and fluorine gas.

....
[2]

b) What type of bonding exists in the product of this reaction?

....
[1]

c) Would you expect the product of this reaction to have a high or low melting point?
Explain your answer in terms of the forces within the compound.

....

....

....

....
[2]
[Total 5 marks]

9 Chlorine water reacts with potassium iodide solution according to the following reaction.

Grade 6-7

$$Cl_{2\,(aq)} + 2KI_{(aq)} \rightarrow 2KCl_{(aq)} + I_{2\,(aq)}$$

a) Describe what you would observe if you added chlorine water to potassium iodide solution.

....
[1]

b) Explain why this reaction takes place.
Give your answer in terms of the reactivity of the elements involved.

....

....
[2]

c) Write a balanced ionic equation for the reaction between chlorine and potassium iodide.

....
[2]

d) Write balanced half equations to show what happens to chlorine and potassium
during this reaction. Use e^- to represent an electron.

Chlorine: ....

Potassium: ....
[2]
[Total 7 marks]

Mixed Questions

10 A scientist wants to produce a batch of aluminium sulfate for an experiment.
She plans to do this by reacting aluminium with an excess of sulfuric acid.
A chemical supplier offers three options to provide the quantity of aluminium she needs.

Which of these options will allow the scientist to complete her reaction in the **shortest** time?

A   1 aluminium cube with side length 8 cm.
B   8 aluminium cubes, each with side length 4 cm.
C   64 aluminium cubes, each with side length 2 cm.
D   They will all take the same length of time.

Your answer ☐

[Total 1 mark]

11 Aluminium can be obtained by electrolysis of the ore bauxite, Al_2O_3.

The overall equation for this reaction is:

$$2Al_2O_{3\,(l)} \rightarrow 4Al_{(l)} + 3O_{2\,(g)}$$

a) Explain why this reaction is an example of a redox reaction.

....

....

[1]

b) Before the electrolysis of aluminium ore can be carried out, the bauxite needs to be molten.
Explain why this is necessary.

....

....

....

[2]

c) Iron can be extracted from its ores by heating with carbon.
Explain why this method is **not** suitable for the extraction of aluminium from its ore.

....

....

....

....

[2]

d) Give **two** advantages of recycling aluminium.

1. ....

....

2. ....

....

[2]

[Total 7 marks]

Mixed Questions

12 Some elements have several different isotopes. Look at the bar chart.
It shows the percentage of the atoms of some elements that exist as each of their isotopes.

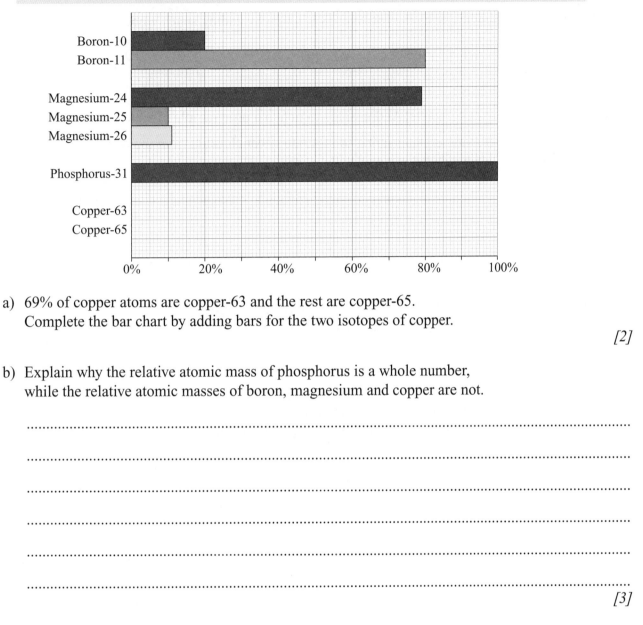

a) 69% of copper atoms are copper-63 and the rest are copper-65.
Complete the bar chart by adding bars for the two isotopes of copper.

[2]

b) Explain why the relative atomic mass of phosphorus is a whole number,
while the relative atomic masses of boron, magnesium and copper are not.

....

....

....

....

....

....

[3]

c) One mole of boron atoms contains 6.022×10^{23} atoms.
How many boron-10 atoms would you expect to find in one mole of boron atoms?
Give your answer to **three** significant figures.

.... atoms

[2]

d) The atomic number of magnesium is 12. Magnesium forms ions with a 2+ charge.
How many electrons are there in one Mg^{2+} ion? Explain your answer.

....

....

....

[2]

[Total 9 marks]

Mixed Questions

13 Andre wants to prepare a sample of silver chloride, AgCl, an insoluble salt.
To do this, he mixes solutions of barium chloride, $BaCl_2$, and silver nitrate, $AgNO_3$.

a) Complete the following equation for Andre's reaction by adding state symbols.

$$BaCl_2(............) + 2AgNO_3(............) \rightarrow 2AgCl(............) + Ba(NO_3)_2(............)$$

[1]

b) When the reaction is complete, Andre wants to obtain a pure sample of silver chloride.

i) Andre suggests using crystallisation to separate silver chloride from the reaction mixture.
Explain why this would be an **unsuitable** method.

....

....

....

[2]

ii) Suggest a suitable method Andre could use to obtain a pure
sample of silver chloride from the reaction mixture.

....

[1]

c) Calculate the atom economy of Andre's reaction.
Give your answer to an appropriate number of significant figures.

.....................................%

[4]

d) By using a suitable method to separate the mixture, Andre obtains 21.51 g of silver chloride.
Given that he started with a solution containing 33.98 g of silver nitrate,
calculate his percentage yield of silver chloride.

.....................................%

[5]

[Total 13 marks]

14 The atomic number of every atom of a certain element, X, is the same. The value of the atomic number is equal to the relative atomic mass of X. Which of the following statements must be **true** for element X?

A Atoms of element X contain no neutrons.
B Element X only has one isotope.
C Atoms of element X have a full outer electron shell.
D Atoms of element X have an equal number of protons and neutrons.

Your answer ☐

[Total 1 mark]

15 The Haber process is used in industry to make ammonia, using the following exothermic reaction.

$$N_{2(g)} + 3H_{2(g)} \rightleftharpoons 2NH_{3(g)}$$

a) What does the '$\rightleftharpoons$' symbol tell you about this reaction?

....

[1]

b)* The Haber process is usually carried out at a pressure of 200 atm and a temperature of 450 °C. Explain why these conditions are considered a compromise. Give your answer in terms of the rate of reaction, equilibrium position and cost.

....

....

....

....

....

....

....

....

....

....

....

....

....

[6]

[Total 7 marks]

16 A hydrogen-oxygen fuel cell is a type of electrical cell.
Hydrogen-oxygen fuel cells produce energy from a redox reaction.

The equation for the reaction is:

$$2H_2 + O_2 \rightarrow 2H_2O$$

a) Which of the following best describes what happens at each electrode in the fuel cell?

A Hydrogen is reduced at the negative electrode and oxygen is oxidised at the positive electrode.
B Hydrogen is oxidised at the negative electrode and oxygen is reduced at the positive electrode.
C Oxygen is reduced at the negative electrode and hydrogen is oxidised at the positive electrode.
D Oxygen is oxidised at the negative electrode and hydrogen is reduced at the positive electrode.

Your answer ☐

[1]

b) The table below shows the energy of the bonds involved in this reaction.

Bond	Bond Energy (kJ/mol)
O=O	498
H–H	436
O–H	463

Calculate the energy change for the reaction which takes place in the hydrogen-oxygen fuel cell.

.... kJ/mol
[3]

c) A fuel cell was is supplied with a limited quantity of hydrogen gas and an excess of oxygen gas.
The quantity of hydrogen used occupied 156 dm³ at room temperature and pressure.
Calculate the amount of energy produced if all of the hydrogen reacted.

.... kJ
[3]
[Total 7 marks]

Mixed Questions

17 Hydrochloric acid, HCl, reacts with aluminium.
The reaction produces aluminium chloride, $AlCl_3$, and hydrogen gas.

$$6HCl_{(aq)} + 2Al_{(s)} \rightarrow 2AlCl_{3\,(aq)} + 3H_{2\,(g)}$$

Calculate the volume of hydrogen gas produced when
162 g of aluminium is added to an excess of hydrochloric acid.
Assume the reaction takes place at room temperature and pressure.

.... dm^3

[Total 3 marks]

18 A scientist carries out an experiment to investigate the rate of reaction between zinc and hydrochloric acid. He prepares three different blocks of zinc metal. The table below shows some information about the three blocks of zinc.

	length (cm)	width (cm)	height (cm)	surface area (cm^2)	volume (cm^3)
Block X	60	1	1	242	60
Block Y	15	2	2	128	60
Block Z	5	3	4	94	60

Which block of zinc would you expect to react **more quickly**?
Explain your answer.

....

....

....

....

....

....

[Total 2 marks]

Mixed Questions

19 Boron nitride, BN, is a compound which can form giant covalent structures. Two forms of boron nitride are shown below.

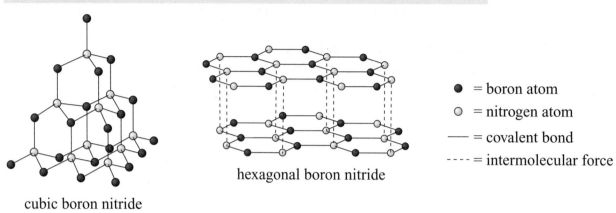

cubic boron nitride

hexagonal boron nitride

● = boron atom
○ = nitrogen atom
— = covalent bond
---- = intermolecular force

a) One of the two forms of boron nitride shown above is used to make drill bits.
The other can be used as a lubricant. Using your knowledge of similar giant covalent structures to suggest which is which, complete the following sentences using either 'cubic' or 'hexagonal'.

i) .... boron nitride is used to make cutting tools.

ii) .... boron nitride is used as a lubricant.

[1]

b) Explain why the structure of boron nitride you have suggested in part a) i) would make it suitable to use to make drill bits.

....

....

....

....

[2]

c) Explain why the structure of boron nitride you have suggested in part a) ii) makes it suitable to use as a lubricant.

....

....

....

....

[2]

d) The main difference between the properties of hexagonal boron nitride and the closest equivalent carbon structure is that hexagonal boron nitride cannot conduct electricity, but its carbon equivalent can. What does this difference suggest about the structure of hexagonal boron nitride?

....

....

[1]

[Total 6 marks]

Mixed Questions